SO-ABD-743

Praise for

YOU BE
YOU

"To truly transform your life—mind, body, and soul—
you must be willing to put in the work. I've seen
Drew Canole put in the work for years to get to
where he is, and this book will guide you to
overcome your limitations as well."

— **Lewis Howes**, *New York Times* best-selling author
of *The School of Greatness*

"Drew's commitment to total-living wellness inspires
the world to embrace our overall health with
greater passion and a renewed commitment
to self. I'm forever grateful."

— **Matt Kahn**, author of *Everything Is Here to Help You*

"Results speak for themselves. Drew has already
impacted the lives of millions of people in a
meaningful way. But what many people hadn't
seen was the inner work he did to be the
person who provides so much outer value.
In *You Be You*, Drew will show you how to tap
into your own brilliance, own your awesome,
and live the life you deserve."

— **Shawn Stevenson**, best-selling author of *Sleep Smarter*

"*You Be You* carries not only an important message for our time, but I believe ultimately the only message that will actually lead us to the transformation and results we all desire deep down. Drew's willingness to be vulnerable gives us permission to release our fears and shame around our stories and instead see how they can be the most powerful thing we can use to step into our authentic path. Drew is one of the most loving, bold, and brilliant leaders of our time, and he is a voice and example of how embracing every part of ourselves and owning our darkness can lead us to the brightest version of ourselves. I am honored to call Drew a friend and can say that every time I spend time with him I gain some sort of wisdom or freedom to become even more me, and that is the ultimate gift."

— **Lori Harder**, top 100 podcast host, transformational coach, fitness world champion, and best-selling author of *A Tribe Called Bliss*

"*You Be You* is a book that gives you unapologetic permission to show up in your greatest expression for who you are. The guidelines laid out will give you the cellular tools to un-layer to your magic."

— **Danette May**, founder of Mindful Health, LLC, certified fitness professional, Pilates instructor, nutritionist, and best-selling author of *Bikini Body Recipes*

"Drew has a way of connecting a person to their innermost self in a way that I've never seen before. He is the perfect person to write this book to help you align and transform into who you're meant to be."

— **Amanda Bucci**, entrepreneur and influencer

YOU BE
YOU

Hay House Titles of Related Interest

YOU CAN HEAL YOUR LIFE, the movie,
starring Louise Hay & Friends
(available as a 1-DVD program, an expanded
2-DVD set, and an online streaming video)
Learn more at www.hayhouse.com/louise-movie

THE SHIFT, the movie,
starring Dr. Wayne W. Dyer
(available as a 1-DVD program, an expanded
2-DVD set, and an online streaming video)
Learn more at www.hayhouse.com/the-shift-movie

❖ ❖ ❖

*CLAIM YOUR POWER: A 40-Day Journey to Dissolve
the Hidden Blocks That Keep You Stuck and Finally
Thrive in Your Life's Unique Purpose,* by Mastin Kipp

*HIGH PERFORMANCE HABITS:
How Extraordinary People Become That Way,*
by Brendon Burchard

*THE TAPPING SOLUTION FOR MANIFESTING YOUR
GREATEST SELF: 21 Days to Releasing Self-Doubt,
Cultivating Inner Peace, and Creating a Life You Love,*
by Nick Ortner

*THE UNIVERSE HAS YOUR BACK:
Transform Fear to Faith,* by Gabrielle Bernstein

All of the above are available at your local bookstore,
or may be ordered by visiting:

Hay House USA: www.hayhouse.com®
Hay House Australia: www.hayhouse.com.au
Hay House UK: www.hayhouse.co.uk
Hay House India: www.hayhouse.co.in

YOU BE YOU

Detox Your Life,

Crush Your Limitations,

and Own Your Awesome

DREW CANOLE

HAY HOUSE, INC.
Carlsbad, California • New York City
London • Sydney • New Delhi

Copyright © 2018 by Fit Life TV LLC

Published in the United States by: Hay House, Inc.: www.hayhouse.com®•
Published in Australia by: Hay House Australia Pty. Ltd.: www.hayhouse
.com.au • *Published in the United Kingdom by:* Hay House UK, Ltd.: www
.hayhouse.co.uk • *Published in India by:* Hay House Publishers India: www
.hayhouse.co.in

Cover design: Ploy Siripant • *Interior design:* Nick C. Welch

All rights reserved. No part of this book may be reproduced by any mechanical, photographic, or electronic process, or in the form of a phonographic recording; nor may it be stored in a retrieval system, transmitted, or otherwise be copied for public or private use—other than for "fair use" as brief quotations embodied in articles and reviews—without prior written permission of the publisher.

The author of this book does not dispense medical advice or prescribe the use of any technique as a form of treatment for physical, emotional, or medical problems without the advice of a physician, either directly or indirectly. The intent of the author is only to offer information of a general nature to help you in your quest for emotional, physical, and spiritual well-being. In the event you use any of the information in this book for yourself, the author and the publisher assume no responsibility for your actions.

To protect the privacy of others, certain names and details have been changed.

Library of Congress has cataloged the earlier edition as follows:

Names: Canole, Drew, author.
Title: You be you : detox your life, crush your limitations, and own your
    awesome / Drew Canole.
Description: 1st edition. | Carlsbad, Calif. : Hay House, [2018]
Identifiers: LCCN 2018034063 | ISBN 9781401955762 (hardcover : alk.
paper)
Subjects: LCSH: Self-realization.
Classification: LCC BF637.S4 C345 2018 | DDC 158.1--dc23 LC record avail-
able at https://lccn.loc.gov/2018034063

Tradepaper ISBN: 978-1-4019-5578-6
E-book ISBN: 978-1-4019-5577-9
Audiobook ISBN: 978-1-4019-5579-3

10 9 8 7 6 5 4 3 2 1
1st edition, October 2018
2nd edition, June 2020

Printed in the United States of America

I'd like to acknowledge my parents, Jeff and Connie Canole, for keeping me grounded and on path. Also, to my mentor Frank Shideler, for being an interruption of love and light on this journey.

CONTENTS

INTRODUCTION

Welcome to *You Be You*! I'm excited that you're joining me. If you're here, it's because you're ready for a transformation. You may not even know it yet, but it's true. Something has led you to this exact moment, so embrace it. Your higher self is encouraging you to shift in one way or another. And that's exciting. Scary? Possibly. But I am here to walk with you on this journey. Somewhere deep inside you, or maybe just beneath the surface, your authentic self—your light, your true essence—is looking for a way out into the Universe. This light, I believe, has been your true purpose since before you were even born. Because of the limitations that have been piled onto you, some by accident and some intentionally, perhaps you haven't yet found a way to embrace and truly own that light.

You've attracted this book into your life because you're ready to begin the journey that will put an end to those limitations and let all that light exude from every part of your being. This book will take you through your very own personal transformation.

I want to be clear, though—it isn't going to be easy. Like anything worth doing, it's going to take commitment and work to get the results you're seeking. You've probably heard the saying *There's no reward without risk*, and that is exactly the idea I am encouraging you to embrace.

I am going to show you how to crush all that programming you've gotten so comfortable with, which has been keeping your bright inner light dimmed, perhaps since you were a child, or maybe even since before you were born. If you commit to this process, though, and follow the exercises in this book with intention and focus, you'll learn not only to live in and own your incredible brilliant light, but also to share it with the world.

How do I know this? Because at our core, we are one. We come from the same Source. We are full of the same light. Your journey is also my journey. You will never have to do this alone. We're in this together . . . more than you and I will ever know. I want you to think of me as a brother, a friend, a coach—whatever works for you. As you read this, know that I am with you as your guide.

My Life's Beginnings

Before I dive in and tell you about my own journey, I want to remind you of a very important truth: while we don't always have control over our circumstances, especially those we may have faced in our younger years, we do have the power to shift our perception of them in a way that allows us to move forward with courage. And although my own journey entailed wounds I am still working to fully heal, I have also embraced the fact that it's okay not to have it all figured out. Instead of shaming myself or beating myself up for things not being perfect, I chose to allow my mess to become my mission.

The moment I decided there absolutely *had* to be a reason I experienced so much pain and anguish at such a young, impressionable age was the moment the whole world shifted and I began to see and feel my personal transformation take shape. I believe this is possible for you too. You see, I believe you are here for a reason. I believe we are sharing space on this planet—in whatever dimension you happen to be right now—intentionally. No accidents.

Some people believe they come into this life by sheer happenstance. I like to believe that we choose our beginnings and that I chose mine for a very specific reason. Yes, I was born into an abusive home. I was neglected and physically tortured. My biological father had a temper, and when he was in a rage, he would do some unthinkable things, like putting cigarettes out on my forehead if I didn't tie my shoes fast enough. There were times when he would hold me underwater, and if I cried when he pulled me out, he would shove me right back under as a way to teach me to "be tough." It was terrible. Yet deep in my soul, I knew there had to be more to life, and in the quiet space when I was alone, even as a very young boy, I prayed for safety. I prayed for love. I prayed for acceptance. And my prayers were ultimately answered.

One day when I was five and my sister was four, we were left alone at home. My sister used this opportunity to jump out a window and run across the street to tell a neighbor about the horrible conditions we were living in. Our neighbor lovingly took us in as she called the authorities. We were pulled from everything we knew—our own messed-up "normal" became a distant memory—and we were immediately placed in foster care, which, sadly, wasn't much of an improvement. Our family programming hadn't given me the tools I desperately needed to be part of society, and my foster parents didn't have the tools to help me. I was whipped for my behavior and had my mouth washed out with soap for my language. I felt damaged and completely unlovable.

I vividly remember questioning God as to why this was my life. But I am clear now that it was actually perfect. Because, despite all the turmoil of those early years, this was the very path that would teach me to create *more* in my life—more love, more independence, more acceptance, more joy. It taught me to be adaptable and to pivot toward positivity instead of fear. More importantly, it taught me forgiveness.

After a year of struggling in foster care, my sister and I were adopted by an amazing family. Divine intervention at its finest! Our adoptive mother had cervical cancer, which prevented her from having her own biological children, the one thing she wanted most in life. Her heartache was what led her to find us, broken children with a desire to be loved. This was no coincidence. The synchronicity of the Universe, or God, if you prefer, delivered us into her life, and vice versa. Our new family was deeply compassionate and sensitive to our needs as abused kids, and we began to steadily heal over the next couple of years. But it was not an easy road. It was only the beginning of a lifelong journey for all of us—a reinvention of "normal" in a way that felt safe, secure, and peaceful.

I remember praying one night, asking God to watch over my mom and dad, my grandma and grandpa, my hamster, rabbit, gerbil, and goldfish, and I remember I prayed to God for the ability to forgive my biological father for everything he had done. I don't know where the knowledge came from, but I knew with every part of me that by forgiving him I could be free.

I now realize I chose the path of those early years to prepare myself for all the circumstances and events when I would need a capacity for radical forgiveness and acceptance—not only of others, but of myself as well. Because of this realization, I can see that anything that may come into my experience is an aspect of myself that I generate and bring into reality. I truly believe I am the one who's actually creating each experience in my life. I don't see another person or circumstance wronging me; I actually see that I am wronging myself. The other side of that, of course, is that when you do right for somebody else, you are actually doing right for yourself. And instead of seeing myself as separate from others, I now understand that in every moment, I have the opportunity to lift up my experience by encouraging and empowering others to do the same. I'm not claiming that one little prayer session brought me into complete, harmonious alignment with Source—far from it! I still had much to learn. In fact, I still do. But it was a start and a shift that would radically and forever transform the way I moved through life.

Who I Am Now

A whole lot went on in the decades between then and now, obviously, and I'll get into much of it as we go through the transformation process in the following pages so you can witness the unfolding of my own transformation as you work on yours. But before all that, let me tell you who I am today in hopes that it will inspire and empower your journey, no matter where you've been.

I founded a health transformation company called Fitlife.tv and a few years later co-founded an organic superfoods company called Organifi in San Diego. Fitlife.tv came first, growing out of a series of videos I shot on health and wellness when I first arrived in California, more than seven years ago now. These videos, which revolved around my own transformation journey, found their way to millions of viewers, and the next thing I knew, I had a whole team producing videos on a weekly (sometimes even daily) basis and taking on clients who were looking to transform their bodies and minds.

After about a year, my small team and I got serious about the next steps for making physical health something the entire world could access. It took about two years of brainstorming and development to come up with the formulation for our flagship product, Organifi Green Juice, an organic superfood blend that fuels people's cells and is also delicious! And now, seven years later, we've got millions of followers who watch our videos and we've developed multiple products to make nutrition easy and accessible, with more ideas in the works. Our mission is to *unite the world in health and happiness,* and we have no plans to slow down.

As part of our work, we've helped millions find their way to the highest version of themselves through our free content and quality products. We have spent years coaching clients both in group settings and one-on-one, and although we no longer directly coach clients, we are still committed to bringing the tools we know to be effective for positive personal transformation to a broader audience. That's partly why I wrote this book. I truly want transformation to be something that feels attainable to everyone, because it is! And having a tribe of others on the same mission who are excited to do the work and create change is one of the best motivators out there. This isn't just about reading encouraging statements and eating healthy, though. Our diet choices are a symptom of much deeper issues, both personal and societal. The reason our community has had so much success is because of our approach, which is to dig, dig, and dig some more until we get to the very heart of the underlying unhappiness. Only then is true, permanent transformation possible.

The Problem Facing People Today

Simply put, a great many of us are not living our truth. It begins early, with our truth being overridden by programming from our parents, and then our teachers, and then our peers and society as a whole. By the time we begin to make significant decisions about our life directions, we've had years of pressure, years of meeting others' expectations, years of doing our best to please others and forgetting about what we really want and need to thrive. In many cases our true selves are buried so far beneath others' expectations that we have little hope of making decisions that truly align with our authentic desires. We've forgotten who we are.

The combination of the Internet, smartphones, and social media only makes things worse. We're constantly bombarded with the latest celebrity news and reminded of how amazing everyone else's life seems, and we've come to rely on positive feedback on our Facebook and Instagram posts to figure out how much our lives are worth. We're in a never-ending external search for happiness, seeking permission from others to be ourselves and be happy, or at least appear to be. In fact, many of us look for acceptance from others before looking inward and accepting ourselves.

As a result of the daily compulsion to be liked and valued by others, we end up in an endless cycle of people pleasing, leaving us empty and unfulfilled. We say yes when we want to say no. We push our true selves down even farther, rather than establishing boundaries and standing up for ourselves and what we know to be true in order to live in harmony with Source. And while our digital circle of "friends" continues to grow, climbing into the hundreds and thousands on social media, how many of them are actual friends? How many of them have any idea who we really are? How could they, if *we* don't even know who we are?

All this has come together to create lonely existences, inauthentic lives, and a widening gap between what's real and what isn't. We've gotten to be experts in covering up our emptiness with the illusion of happiness. But we remember just enough of our childhood innocence and freedom to realize there's more to life than this constant need for validation. What we really want is the experience of truth, of integrity, of living in the brilliance of our true light. We want that innocence and freedom back, but we don't know how to get it.

Many people in our community come to us having already read hundreds of books. They've tried dozens of programs and diets, cleanses and workouts, but they haven't gotten the results they really want because they're doing these things for the wrong reasons. They're doing them because society tells them they should be a certain weight or they should strive for a particular job or they should live in a particular place—none of which aligns with who they are at the core.

The solution for this is nothing short of individual transformation. We must each undertake a personal journey to strip away all those limiting expectations and societal pressures so we can reveal our authentic selves and live in the light of who we really are. When this is achieved, our decisions come into alignment with our true selves and we begin to attract things to us that resonate with a frequency that feels good and right. This happens in relationships, health goals, career directions, and everything else we desire.

The Transformation Journey

This transformation is a three-part process. Part I, "Detox Your Life," is about preparation—the preparation of your mind, body, and soul for the difficult middle stretch of the journey. We'll take a look at the habits and belief systems that have been holding you back and give you powerful tools to detox your life—to commit to change, discover your true purpose, and examine the way you treat your body.

Part II, "Crush Your Limitations," is about getting honest and identifying—and then crushing—your self-limiting beliefs, many of which have been placed upon you through conditioning from your parents, teachers, friends, and society in general. Some of these beliefs, you'll find, have one heck of a hold on you, and will require you to face some serious dragons before you can proceed, but never fear—I'll give you what you need to do just that. Remember, I've walked that walk myself.

Part III is "Own Your Awesome"—your unique light, your worth, your individuality, the very thing that makes you *you*. This means developing the awareness to immediately recognize when something is in alignment with your true frequency and having the confidence to reject everything else with the knowledge that you are already abundant. It means having the tools to create and maintain serious momentum for yourself, the kind that can't help but sweep others into its power and its positivity.

An Overview of My Mission

My mission is to provide you with the tools—the belief, the commitment, the steps—to empower you to undertake your own personal journey to authenticity. The tools necessary for you to come home to yourself, to the person you were so carefully crafted to be in this world. First, I want you to grant yourself permission to be *you* and nobody but you. By doing so I am confident you will begin to remember who you really are and what you're here to do. With this newfound realization, you will start showing up in the world as the person you've been all along—just brighter and ready to shine.

You'll stop relying on those external ideas, standards, and expectations you've been conditioned with, and you'll grow beyond all the accompanying programs, books, diets, and advice. Instead, you'll tap into Source, the natural energy within you, which starts to flow through you when you step in and own it with the radical acceptance of who you are at your core. Sound familiar, *Star Wars* fans? That's right—I'm talking about showing up like a Jedi. You are that powerful. You'll begin to inhabit a place of flow, where there is a constant renewal of energy. Rather than depleting you, your daily circumstances will instead strengthen you, and you will find yourself continually leveling up, so your frequency, your awesome, can shine through everything you do and every life you touch, brighter than ever before.

This is the mission I have dedicated my transformed life to in creating Fitlife.tv and Organifi, and now this book, which is a constant reminder of our human capacity and ability to level up and focus out in everything that we do. And while I've shared my secrets with millions of people in our community over the last several years, never before have I been so explicit and comprehensive about the secrets that guide us toward happiness and fulfillment. But this journey isn't about me—it's about you. Truthfully, it's about *us* and about recognizing, accepting, and loving the oneness we can attain when we live as our authentic selves.

The Benefits You Can Expect

Once you've detoxed your life, crushed your limitations, and owned your awesome, you'll upgrade how you show up and you'll be more aligned with what you want most: more happiness, more peace, more creative energy, more love. You'll have a radical new perspective that will dissolve any darkness—anything not serving your highest self—and instead be infused with your unique and beautiful light. You'll develop a new mind-set, learning to drop any resistance you have to your true self as you willingly and openly surrender to the support of the Universe. Furthermore, you'll learn to trust that the Universe has your back. If you believe and take action, the Universe will meet you halfway. You'll learn how to get honest with yourself—without judgment—and you'll learn to maintain that feel-good space you've cultivated with meditation and positive intention. You'll take a kinder stance in accepting yourself, and therefore a kinder, more accepting stance toward others. You'll learn to keep your inner critics in check and get out from beneath their judgment. I can tell you from experience that they won't disappear entirely—I've still got about eight of them, and they all speak with different accents! Sometimes they argue with each other when I'm in the shower, and when they've had their say, I acknowledge them, thank them, and then remind them I don't need them anymore. You won't be able to silence the external expectations completely, but they'll no longer cast a dark cloud over your authentic self. The result of this will be greater freedom, happiness, and abundance in your life.

What This Book Is *Not*

This is not a book about setting goals—although it will help you develop the tools you need to uncover and attain your deepest desires.

This is not a weight-loss book—although if you authentically desire to lose weight, you will learn how to do it. While my business background involves juicing, this isn't a juicing book—although we'll talk at length about how your body is an important entry point to transformation and how it's critical to the process to be in harmony with your body on a cellular level.

This book isn't a miracle solution—there's no such thing. Rather, you'll be given the opportunity to commit to putting in the work and stretching yourself each and every day in order to achieve results.

Finally, this isn't a sugarcoated version of the journey. It's about *embracing* the mess and then creating a mission that has you jumping out of bed in the morning with a newfound sense of purpose and joy in everything you do and everyone you meet.

What This Book Is, and How to Use It

This book is about commitment to a journey. *Your* journey. The program I've laid out here is actually pretty simple, but that doesn't mean it will be easy. I'm taking you down the rabbit hole to places that might feel scary and uncomfortable. But remember, nothing of value comes without effort. And in this case, that effort will carry you through the intensity and the messiness to a place of beauty and peace, the place you've been seeking—the place that already exists inside you.

It's best if you commit fully from the beginning. Really get into this process. Set a firm intention to read each page with an open heart, giving every exercise a shot and even trying them multiple times if that's what it takes for them to stick. Keep a journal and write about your experiences as you go. If you can, recruit an accountability partner to go on the journey with you. I don't know about you, but I believe there is power in numbers, and I find I am much more successful when I have someone to help me stay on track. You can share notes and lift each other up when things get tough, and you can celebrate together when you have breakthroughs!

Throughout the book there are thought experiments and mind-set-shifting exercises that will help you integrate the concepts in each chapter into your everyday life. For the full benefit of transformation, plan to do each exercise with your full focus, making every attempt to participate as your authentic self. Not only will you learn more about yourself, but you'll begin the practice of operating from your true desires—which is the ultimate goal.

Life-changing transformation awaits you on the following pages. Sometimes it'll be fun and easy; other times it'll be difficult and uncomfortable. If you approach this process with full commitment and compassion for yourself, you'll not only realize a complete transformation but also enjoy the journey. I've done it myself; I've seen it work for others; and I know it's there for you too. We're in this together. Let's go!

PART I

Detox Your Life

Welcome to the first stage of the journey! You've taken trips before, right? Before you even head out of the house, you've wrapped up things at work and in your everyday life—you've tidied up, found someone to feed the cat, maybe changed your outgoing voice mail message or set up an e-mail auto reply. You've checked and rechecked that the windows are locked and the stove is off, and you've made sure there are going to be no big surprises waiting for you in the fridge when you get back (veggie-lover problems). You've made some reservations, whether booking a flight or hotel or a rental car. You've got a dog-eared guidebook to the places you want to visit.

The point is, you did a ton of thinking, planning, and acting before you started your trip, and this journey is no different. In fact, I encourage you to think of that preparation as part of the journey itself. A huge part of the pleasure of travel is the anticipation and planning, as I'm sure you've experienced!

This is a different kind of journey, but it requires the same attention to preparation. Part I focuses on three areas we'll work to prepare and detox together: mind, body, and soul. Chapter 1 covers the first and most important step of any journey: commitment. And this is not just a commitment on paper—we'll work to create a feeling that reaches into your subconscious, a powerful change that will begin to create what you want in your life. In Chapter 2 we'll take a deep dive into the concept of "whydentity." I think of this as "the why that makes you cry." It's your deepest, most authentic purpose—it's your reason for being and doing on this planet. It's not the reason crafted for you by teachers and parents and advertising, but the reason that's so true to you it will make you unstoppable. Chapter 3, the final stage of the preparation and detox process, is about honoring your body. Are your daily choices—for mind, body, and spirit—creating the best foundation for an authentic, purpose-driven life? Or could you be creating a better way for the new you to flourish?

The work you'll do in this first part isn't always going to be easy, but diligence and care on your part will create a strong foundation for the later stages, where you'll encounter and battle all the things that have been holding you back and keeping your light dim. So get comfortable, get ready, and let's prepare together for the most transformative journey you could ever take—the journey to your highest and best self.

Chapter 1

COMMIT TO YOURSELF

Your entire transformation from limited to full of light begins with a small but incredibly powerful step: commitment. I remember the exact moment of my own commitment. I was in Tampa Bay, watching the waves come in one beautiful late afternoon, thinking about my life and purpose, when suddenly everything shifted.

At the time I had been running a financial services company I'd founded two years earlier, when I was just out of college, helping people get out of debt. By this time I'd developed a natural flair for enrolling people in my vision and my mission, so the business was a big success—by my old standards, anyway. But I was still carrying around a lack of love from my early years with my biological parents, and I had come to believe on a subconscious level that my financial success would make people love me more and fill what I thought of as a big void within. I was chasing money, and I had caught it. I had the cars, the watches, the women, the house. I'd created a vision, and it worked—until it didn't.

What didn't work was the lifestyle I was living. I was going out every weekend and drinking copious amounts of alcohol in order to escape what I had buried and continuously tried to forget about, pretending that the life I'd built was okay. At the end of those two years, I was 40 pounds overweight, unhappy in my own skin, and so far removed from who I truly was that I began to feel unrecognizable when I looked in the mirror. Who had I become? And where was the real Drew? I was doing everything I could to mask the pain from my childhood and put on a front in hopes it would all somehow fix itself.

The truth, however, was that my lifestyle was completely out of alignment with who I knew I was deep down, at my core. Despite my best efforts to ignore my past and embrace my "successful" life, I had never felt more separate from Source—and from myself. It's hard for me to believe now that I did that every weekend, without fail, despite how bad it made me feel. And in Tampa Bay that afternoon, when I really got honest with myself about where I'd be heading if I stayed on this path, it terrified me to think that this could be it—unless I made some serious changes.

It was at this time that I also began to notice there were others around me who didn't care about monetary success. In fact, I knew people who were deeply happy doing what they loved, and everything else in their lives seemed to be falling into place. I began to realize that in order to feel the way I wanted to, I had to embrace a new reality. This meant changing my current way of being— and getting uncomfortable in the process.

A few months earlier, I had met Frank, who was to become one of my greatest mentors. He was hosting a large Thanksgiving dinner which I'd been invited along to, though I knew very few of the others there. I'd never met him before, but he greeted me at the door with a hug. And it wasn't just any hug—it was a warm, extended hug like he was remembering me from long, long ago, like I was family. And as I looked into his brilliant blue eyes, I felt immediately safe and at home. Frank is extremely intuitive, and he could feel my anxiety in stepping into a new space with strangers. Instead of throwing me to the wolves, he helped ground me by putting me to work. He realized a task would help me focus outward and begin to settle into my authentic self, which was the very reason I had been provided the opportunity to be in his home in the first place.

After that I had breakfast with Frank almost every day for two years while living in Florida. He taught me about love, about giving, about blessing. He taught me about what it really meant to live with purpose. He helped me shift so that I finally felt my business was aligned with my true self. I had shared my struggles about the type of work I was doing and let him know I felt called to really help people, and he told me something I will never forget. He told me I was in the blessing business, and instead of focusing inward and solely on the numbers—that is, on what I was gaining personally from the work I was doing—it was time that I began looking for people to bless each and every day. He told me, "If you're doing anything at all, make sure you're doing something to change somebody's life." Hearing this was the permission I didn't know I had needed, and it lit a fire in my belly, creating a stir inside that I had never quite felt before. I followed Frank's advice, and I never looked back.

I'll get back to my transformation-in-progress in just a moment, but I want to hit pause on my own story and turn the camera around to ask you, Has your life come to a similar crossroads? Are you—subconsciously or consciously—waiting for a similar encounter, for a similar act of permission to nudge you down a different pathway? Maybe you've been suspecting for some time that there's a different, higher version of yourself out there, but you've been having trouble believing there's a real pathway to get you there. If that's the case, it is my greatest hope at this point in our journey together that my story and this book could act as the kind of permission for you that Frank provided for me. Of course, I can't see the specifics of your life, but consider this: Something brought this book into your life. Whether a friend loaned it to you or you read about it somewhere or it simply caught your eye at the bookstore, some desire you were putting out into the Universe was powerful enough to bring our lives together. So maybe, just maybe, you've already taken that first step toward a new you. With that suggestion in your thoughts, let's keep moving forward—together! Here's how my own story continues:

It was around the same time as my life-altering conversation with Frank that I can vividly remember sitting at the edge of the ocean on a warm Florida afternoon, watching the waves come in, when suddenly a realization came upon me: I wanted to start over. I wanted to live my dream life, to inspire people, to motivate, educate, and entertain people, and to get clear on my life's purpose so I could fulfill it every single day. I was ready to jump in and make my life's work a reality, to truly live out my reason for being on this planet. I finally understood that it didn't matter what I had gone through—I could choose to change direction. The path that was laid out when I had been created was perfect, and the outcome of what I was responsible for contributing to humanity would be so much bigger than me, so much bigger than I ever imagined. I still get chills when I think about how crystal clear this epiphany was. And even though I didn't physically look the part at the time, I knew my calling had something to do with health and total transformation, with a focus on creating positive mind-set shifts within the frameworks of faith and spirituality.

As the waves crashed one after the other, the clarity continued to roll in, and I knew what I would need in order to make this a reality. To give up the business I had built and truly start over, I would need $70,000 as a reserve for six months to a year, if I budgeted right, so I could get a new business off the ground. I didn't think I had anything I could make or offer to generate that kind of cash instantaneously, but I trusted that this calling was real and that it had come directly from a higher power, so instead of cowering in fear, I became determined to fulfill it. I declared that somehow, some way, I would generate $70,000 in the next 30 days and I would use all that I had learned up to this point to create a movement to shift consciousness and the reality of the world as I knew it. I was going to make a positive difference, no matter what. It was time to make my mess my mission and create massive impact in a way I felt aligned with. There was no more time for scarcity or playing small. It was time to rise up and create a ripple effect that would inspire others to do the same.

Can You Relate?

Think back to the way I was living my life in the beginning of this story. In a very literal sense, I was *not myself.* I was allowing the actions of others to limit every piece of my true, authentic self while I was chasing what I thought was love, because my biological parents hadn't shown me that. I was chasing money because in other areas of my life I felt a lack, and somewhere in my subconscious I thought money might be the answer. I was chasing approval because I hadn't yet learned to approve of myself. I wasn't living in alignment with my true purpose, and it was causing me pain—pain that I tried to chase away with material items, shallow relationships, and lots of alcohol and bad food. As a result of these damaging coping mechanisms, my foundation—my body— was in a state of toxicity. And with my body and mind both toxic messes, toxicity was the only possible condition my spirit could dwell in.

I know I am not alone in this. Chances are you are reading this right now and nodding your head because (1) you've been there or (2) you're there right now. And that's *okay*! Maybe your true light has been dimmed by expectations from parents, teachers, or friends, even those who meant well. Maybe you've given up fighting for the life that you know, deep down, you were meant to lead, because you simply don't see how it's possible—especially now. I want to remind you of something though—if this sounds like you at all, know that you're not alone. I believe the vast majority of human souls never manage to break out from beneath the weight of their limiting beliefs and never quite find a way to let their true brilliance shine out into the world, primarily because of *fear*. Wayne Dyer said, in one of my all-time favorite quotations: "Don't die with your music still inside you." My interpretation of this is simple: you were meant to share your passions and your gifts. And if you don't know what they are yet, my hope is that by the end of this book, you will. And you will also have a good idea of how to go after them and live your life with purpose every single day.

My guess is that you're here because you have had about enough of feeling lost or lacking or off-purpose. You are ready to step into the life you were meant to live, with the body and mind you know is somewhere inside you, just begging to be seen and heard. I've been where you are, and truthfully there are still moments when I have to get honest with myself and course-correct. It doesn't just happen—*boom*, you're done, cruise control to happily ever after. The work is constant, and *that* is where the beauty lies.

First, however, you've got to get honest and let go of anything holding you back, anything keeping you from showing up as the *you* that's been somewhere inside there all along. It's time—right now—to detox. Together we are going to clear away the physical toxins that plague your body, the psychological toxins that encumber your mind, and the emotional toxins that burden your spirit. It's time to free yourself, and it all starts with the small but vastly powerful act of commitment.

What does it actually mean to commit? *Commitment* is a word we throw around a lot, often casually. We "commit" to new diets and exercise fads, which often means trying something out for a couple weeks before we get bored or decide it's just not for us. Even our marital commitments, which we declare publicly and often in holy settings, are famously ineffective. I'm talking here about a deeper commitment—a shift throughout every level of your consciousness that will literally transform your vibration and the way you show up in the world so you begin to attract what you truly desire into your experience.

How can this be true? How can making a commitment create a new reality? You are not solely the physical body you see each day in the mirror—your body, though important, is just your meat suit that houses all the beautiful pieces that make up who you intrinsically are at the very core of your existence. You are made of so much more than what the world sees with its eyes. You are made of pure light, a high-vibing frequency with the power to shine out and illuminate everything you are blessed to encounter in the world. And once you commit, you create a powerful resonant condition so that whatever area you're committing to, whether relationships, events, career opportunities, financial situations, or anything else, will begin to flow in a way that feels right.

Exercise: Awesomeness Audit

Over the years many people in the Fitlife.tv community have told me they don't know what they want or what they're supposed to be doing with their life. Some are even worried that through all life's changes, challenges, and surprises, they have lost sight of who they are. There are people like Jessica, who had close friends and a strong marriage but couldn't stand her job and didn't know what else to do. Or Zach (who we'll come back to), who had a happy and stable family life but wasn't treating his body right. These stories are far too common, and by the time people come to us for guidance, they are often so far removed from their authentic selves that they cannot seem to grasp how truly amazing they really are. Helping people come back home to their light is one of my favorite things—and the main inspiration for this book. So let's dig in a bit.

Below is a list of significant areas that make up the life you are currently living. Take a moment and go through and rate each one from 1 to 5, based on how satisfied you are (1 = not satisfied, 5 = extremely satisfied). Do this without judgment—the areas where you feel a lack are the perfect places to start upgrading your life to align with your desires. So get honest! And do it with love. Be sure to write your answers somewhere easily accessible so you can refer back to them later.

- Friends
- Romantic partnership/relationship
- Career
- Finances
- Health/body
- Home/family life
- Spiritual path

Your scores are proportional to the amount of light—the amount of *you*—that's streaming into each of these areas in this very moment. (The best part? This can change at any given moment, should you choose.) So how does it look? Are these areas aligned in a way that feels exciting, inspiring, fulfilling? Or could they use a little nudge to bump them up? Chances are there is at least one area that could use more love and attention, which is great! You're on the right track by reading this book.

Now look at each area and ask yourself: What would your scores look like if life were *easy*? Who would be in your circle of friends? What kind of work would you be doing if money didn't matter? If you could wave a magic wand, what would your health be like? Your family? How would life feel for you if it just flowed?

Who Are You Really?

Have you ever walked into a room and been drawn to someone, or maybe a group of people? This is because of what they're made of—their *light*. You want to be in their presence. You feel good, energized, and on fire in the midst of this light.

You've undoubtedly heard this light called by other names. In China it's called *chi* (or *qi*), and serves as the basis not only for tai chi but also for acupuncture and in fact all of Chinese medicine. Others call it *life force* or *superconsciousness*. *Star Wars* fans, again, will recognize this as our real-life version of the Force. Whatever name resonates with you, the truth is that *you* are a magnificent being placed here in this moment to be part of the creation of the world we live in, in whatever capacity you call forth into your experience. And it's all based on that brilliant light within—the very thing that attracts others to you.

This light is so powerful because it is in all things. It is in every breath you and I take, in every living thing: animals, trees, even rocks. It is our shared oneness, the divine synergy between ourselves and everything else. And when you stop to witness this light, you create a moment of unlimited power with the potential to transform yourself in any way you desire. In that moment you realize your everyday surroundings are an illusion and this light permeates everything on the planet, in every dimension, in every time, all at once, folding it into oneness. This means you are the big bang; you are the cosmos in disguise. I believe that's what Jesus, the Buddha, and all the saints in all the religions were here to teach us.

This idea of the light within you is not merely a poetic way to think of yourself but the foundation for a new way of being, with the power to actually draw the things you want toward you. Think of a simple glow-in-the-dark toy. Because of its unique characteristics, it absorbs light energy from a source, stores it, and then sends it back out. Or think of a guitar showroom. Pluck a string on one guitar hanging on the wall, and the energy of the resulting note will cause the corresponding strings on all the other guitars nearby to begin vibrating with the same sound.

It is the same with your unique light. Since committing to my own transformation, I have seen this in action literally hundreds of times among my friends in the Fitlife.tv community. Once they commit to taking ownership of their light—to doing everything possible to stop resisting it and to let it shine through them and out into the world—their unique frequencies (their gifts!) begin to illuminate pathways they didn't realize existed, at least not for them. Possibilities arise, doors open, and others with similar vibrations appear. As a result of this one little act—commitment—I've seen amazing transformations.

One area where commitment can result in vast improvements is in our relationships. This was the case with John, a 41-year-old tech company V.P., whose marriage had stagnated because of all the attention he had been putting toward work. He and his beautiful wife, Sylvia, together came to the goal of creating more balance, and he carved out quality time with his wife by adding it to his calendar every day. While the scheduling felt far from romantic, John had grown accustomed to living by his calendar and knew this would be a way to start creating a new habit that he could stick to. After just two weeks of this constant reminder, John and Sylvia were scheduling weekly date nights and began rekindling their 13 years of wedded bliss. In fact, 30 days into their new date-night ritual, Sylvia found out they would be expecting their first child. Talk about a serious transformation!

Many of us have had challenging pasts, some containing deeply painful traumas, and are facing a series of more difficult obstacles on the journey into our light.

I remember Jack, a 58-year-old veteran of the Marine Corps, who was struggling to create a positive mind-set and get out of a negativity slump. In his years in the military, Jack had seen some horrific things. He found himself questioning humanity after all the pain and destruction he had seen around the world, and this began showing up in his thoughts in nearly everything he did. He questioned everyone's intentions, began believing he was destined to fail and live a mediocre life, and was plagued with an internal dialogue that had become full of darkness. He understood that he wasn't condemned to a lifetime of such thoughts though, and he was committed to betterment and open to trying new directions. After speaking with him and better understanding when and where these changes in mind-set occurred, we made a plan to begin small, with actionable items that felt realistic, such as daily mantras and a plan to find professional help to address his PTSD and get him back on track. Jack admitted that the mantras felt forced at first, but as he held to his commitment to create new habits and worked on reframing his thoughts, he found himself becoming lighter and happier, and even setting an example for the other veterans in his community. Jack began to feel like himself again after 90 days and was determined to keep it going for, in his words, "as long as it takes!"

Others, of course, are looking for physical transformations. Shelley, who owns a craft store, was 52 when our paths crossed one summer. Her goal that year was to lose 10 pounds and to get off her high-blood-pressure medication, but she'd created a habit of grabbing food on the go while at work, and instead of dropping 10 pounds, she'd added 10, and now had 20 to trim. For her the solution was to eliminate excuses for being "too busy" and to use her weekends to prepare healthy meals to get her through the week. She experienced some challenges and setbacks in the beginning, but after dedicating herself to her health and setting manageable goals, Shelley developed the new habit of taking two hours every Sunday to work in the kitchen with her favorite music on. Four months later, Shelley had lost those 20 pounds and had also added in daily morning walks where she set her intentions for the day and recommitted to herself over and over again.

These are just some of the stories of those who made a commitment to go for it, took radical action to see their dreams actualized, and witnessed the truth that nothing is beyond our grasp when we are open and accepting. Of course, it takes work. For some it even takes a full 180-degree turn to create a completely different way of life. But the commonality in everyone I have had the pleasure of working with is that those who followed through both saw and felt the benefits of their actions, which were met with more love, abundance, prosperity, and peace. And in the process, they discovered their deeper selves, the full brightness of their true light. It's all possible—for you too.

For me this commitment to the discovery and expression of true light means showing up and bringing the highest possible frequency I can muster to all my interactions, even when I'm having an off day. I'm not perfect—like you, I have days that I'd love to do over—but I do try my best to be intentional with every encounter in hopes of leaving people and places better. I make it a goal to spread love, to lift others up, to create experiences with people in a way that inspires more energy, more light, more possibility. Being a catalyst for joy in another's life is not only a choice we get to make every day, it's also *free*. In fact, raising someone else's energy actually helps us raise our own, so it becomes an endless feedback cycle of positivity and connectedness. And because Source is infinite, there's no end to the energy you can tap into if your intention and commitment are strong enough. You have every bit as much capacity to inspire and uplift others as anyone else. When you can channel your light, live your individual purpose, and shine your light back out, others will notice their energy rise, and they'll be motivated, even if it's just on a subconscious level, to do the same.

Own Your Light

Sounds great, right? So why don't more people choose a life of authenticity and light? Simply put: It can be hard. It can be scary. It requires big responsibilities and big vulnerabilities, and more than likely will bring about the largest set of changes and ultimate leaps of faith you've ever experienced. In the words of the brilliant Marianne Williamson: "It is our light, not our darkness, that most frightens us."

So what are these responsibilities I'm talking about? These vulnerabilities? When you take ownership of your light, it means taking full responsibility for all that you are and all that you do. It means no more blaming your parents or your upbringing. No more blaming your boss or your job or your bank balance or your busy schedule. It's all on you now. It's owning your role in every situation and acknowledging that you are ultimately the creator of your experience. The power in this truth is that *you*—yes, *you*—also get to change it.

For me, owning my light and honoring my purpose meant leaving behind a beautiful city, the financial security of a lucrative business, and the familiarity of all my friends. While I knew this was the right decision, it also wasn't easy. And the truth is, you might have to make changes that are just as drastic in your own life. It might be time to say goodbye to some chapters and embrace the unknown. Do your friends' vibrations align with your aspirations? Or do they more often serve as a ready distraction to help you avoid confronting your dissatisfactions? What about your partner? Does your relationship provide the kind of framework that encourages you to develop fully into your utmost purpose? How about the town or city where you live? As you drive or walk around, do you see possibilities for the expansion of your being and the attainment of your highest goals, or do you see worn-out circuits of fast-food restaurants and bars? What about your habits at home: diet, exercise, leisure time?

It's time to leave the old, toxic ways behind. Some of the people in your life will have to go. It might be time to embrace a shift to a new career, a new city, maybe even a new relationship. You can't binge-watch Netflix endlessly anymore while eating garbage and neglecting quality sleep. If you aren't willing to take a hard look at all these areas of your life and evaluate them based not on familiarity and comfort but in the light of true transformation, you're not ready to commit, and you might as well put this book down now.

If you're resisting taking a hard, honest look at yourself but you'd like to overcome that resistance, think of it this way: We're all hurtling through space at 80,000 miles an hour, orbiting a sphere of fire of such power and intensity there's no way for us to comprehend it. An infinity of time stretches out both behind us and before us—and that's only one universe. So all those things—relationships, places, status symbols—you think you're attached to? They're not so critical after all. You're afforded this one small opportunity to *live* and *thrive* and *be happy*, so commit to showing yourself kindness, discovering your light, and letting it flow through you in a way that ignites your spirit and impacts those around you. I am confident you'll be glad you did.

Exercise: Manifest Your Meditations

Grab a sheet of paper and a pen, then begin this exercise with five or ten minutes of meditation. Sit somewhere quiet and peaceful and take a few deep breaths, breathing in through your nose and out through your mouth. If you've ever done yoga, think of how the instructor cues lion's breath. Breathe deep into your belly and let it all go. With each exhalation release your everyday beliefs and attachments. Try to create a blank slate for newness to flourish. Envision the power of your unique light, which has been building up inside you directly from Source, searching for a way out. Once you feel a calm, empowering sensation, return your thoughts to your current reality. Take a look at your career, your relationships, your diet, your exercise routine, your thought patterns . . . you get the idea. Expand your thinking beyond your head—use your whole self, your heart and throat and stomach.

Now make a list of three to five things that are working in your life and a list of three to five things that are *not* working in your life. Take this second list and for each item, write down an outcome that aligns with your authentic self and a statement of commitment to that outcome. For example, if your relationship appears on this list, write, *I choose an enjoyable relationship that feels deeply aligned and in harmony with who I really am*. These are the three to five choices you'll be committing to first. You're creating a vision for your future, gathering the tools you'll use to knock away those obstacles and finally let your light burst out of you.

Finding Your Authentic Flow

Maybe you've heard of "flow" or the "flow state." The flow state is what the basketball player is accessing when he gets so hot he just can't miss a basket, no matter how far out or well-guarded he is. It's the stage actress who so brilliantly channels the character she's playing that she transports the audience completely out of the playhouse and into a fictional realm. It's the concert pianist who performs a piece with such emotion that his audience is reduced to tears.

Good news! The flow state isn't just for star athletes or talented performers—it's accessible to everybody, all the time, including you. My intention with this book is to help you find your own flow state by guiding you home to the authentic life where your light can flow through you as easily as it would flow through a piece of flawless crystal. When you're in a state of flow, it's like an open road where all the lights are green. Difficult things become as easy as breathing, and your movement toward your purpose becomes as fluid and as satisfying as the perfect arc on a three-point shot at the buzzer.

Science has been fascinated with the flow state for quite some time. It has been notoriously difficult to study, because you can't stop a basketball game to attach electrodes to the hottest player, and I'm guessing clusters of eager researchers in white lab coats would probably ruin most stage productions. Scientists have been able to discover, however, that the prefrontal cortex—the foremost part of your brain, just behind your forehead—lights up when you're in a flow state. Why is this significant? The prefrontal cortex is the part of the brain most associated with humanness—it's where our highest levels of creativity, empathy, and spirituality dwell. And it is a place where the two halves of your brain work together. It means you're fully present, fully in the moment. It means you are fully *you*.

To achieve flow, however, you *must* deal with the darkness within. I think of this darkness as the *shadow*. It's in all of us, and it's the part of us that works in opposition to the light. It's the part that thinks it can protect us by keeping us small and inwardly focused. It wants to keep us safe by avoiding risks and hiding from challenges. It wants to evade the pressure of responsibility by dismissing ambition or blaming others. It tells us that sitting on the couch and eating pizza and watching trashy TV all weekend is a substitute for true self-care.

It very often shows up in the form of self-doubt, pieces of which you've picked up over the whole course of your life—from the limiting beliefs of parents, teachers, peers, or anyone else you've allowed to have power over you. All that self-doubt builds up inside you and shows up as obstacles that block the light that wants to be free. In order to find your flow, you've got to face those obstacles, one by one, and love yourself enough to let them go. But how? How do you find your darkness, your shadow, and let it go, and truly let your light shine out into the world?

Often the easiest starting point is to get clear on what isn't working for you. This can be uncomfortable, so you'll have to commit to a policy of radical honesty with yourself. Some of your conclusions might run contrary to the opinions of those you love and value, so you're going to have to tap into your inner warrior spirit. Be brave!

Exercise: Sensory Check

One of the key elements of the flow state is a complete focus on the present moment. So often our minds are filled with thoughts of the past and the future—memories of what happened 20 minutes or 20 years ago, plans and anxieties about the future. This is a simple exercise to help you step out of that pattern and ground yourself in the present. I suggest you do this several times throughout the day, whenever you've got a spare 30 seconds.

First take a deep breath. Let it out. Now do a quick inventory of each of your senses. What images are there, right before you? What time of day is it, and what is the light like? What are you hearing? Are there sounds nearby or far off or both? How does your skin feel? How do your stomach, your lungs, your muscles feel? How does the ground feel beneath your feet? What smells surround you? Are there lingering tastes in your mouth?

Pick out three things from that list of immediate sensations to be grateful for. A nice coolness in the breeze, perhaps, or music from a passing car.

Repeat this exercise as often as you can, and before long it will become effortless—your mind will naturally focus more on the present than on all those racing thoughts of the past and future.

The Power of Commitment

At this point in the process, it's not unusual to feel a little overwhelmed. After all I've just asked you to examine every aspect of your life and consider taking radical action to create massive change. Before we go on, take a moment to ground yourself with this simple reminder, which I believe with all my heart and soul: none of us are accidents. We're all here for a reason, and we are responsible for discovering what that reason—our purpose—is and for doing everything in our power to be the best version of ourselves in order to fulfill it. So yes, you may need to make some shifts that feel uncomfortable, that bring about emotions that don't feel good in the moment. But if your goal is the full attainment of your ultimate, Universe-created, authentic purpose—your true, brilliant light—how much are you going to let a few obstacles slow you down? As I said before, it isn't going to be easy, and it probably won't be straightforward. Either way, though, it starts with commitment.

Now it's time to take the commitments from the exercise in the previous section and fill your entire being with them. There is no halfway point here—there are no test runs, no "giving it a try," because only when you infuse every bit of your body and mind with your full intention will the Universe rise up to meet you. This is why many diets, exercise routines, and other attempts at transformation fail. It's likely you have experienced this yourself at some point. I know I have. Maybe there was a time when you recognized the need for change; perhaps you even identified *how* you were going to change and verbalized that commitment to your friends or family. Maybe you started using a mantra or two and developed a regular habit of repeating them. But what were you actually *doing*? Did you really believe what you were wishing for or working toward was possible? A little nugget of truth for you: anything is possible if you just believe! (Thank you for the wisdom, Jiminy Cricket.)

If that commitment did not reach you at the deepest level possible and fill every ounce of your human self, where it truly had the power to persuade you in every decision and action, then it could not have created the sort of movement and dedication that the Universe recognizes and rewards. Don't give the Universe reason to question you. Be clear with your desires and align your actions so much that the Universe knows without a doubt that you mean business!

With an incomplete commitment, your words, thoughts, feelings, and actions don't match up, and the misalignment keeps you stuck. Remember when Luke was trying to lift his X-wing starfighter from the swamp? He failed because his belief and his commitment weren't wholehearted—because he was merely trying. And remember Yoda's admonition? "There is no try." So true, Yoda. So true.

Take Sara, for example. When I first spoke to Sara, she was worried that her bad habits were being carried over to her children. For her that meant poor choices with food and a lack of motivation to be active. She'd been conditioned to believe food was a great comforter and being active was for "skinny people." Neither belief served her greatest good, and despite knowing this she also had a hard time believing she could change. Sara had a lot of walls up and I wasn't sure she was really ready to do the work necessary to create new habits. I knew it was possible because I had seen it many times over the years, but it had to start with her—nothing I would say or do would be enough.

Sara and I chatted back and forth for a few months. I gave her some exercises to help get her in the right mindset to take on this new lifestyle in a way that would align with her goals and her work schedule, her children's commitments outside of school, and the overall health of her family. She did them on and off, yet in the end, she just wasn't ready to do what it took to go all the way. Instead of dragging her through the process, I let her know that

I believed in her and that when she really felt ready to make the changes necessary and actualize her dream life, she could contact me and I would be more than happy to walk the path with her.

And that's the thing, my friend. Change only happens with *your* commitment to the work. No person or thing will be the magic formula for your own transformation. But at the same time, you get to trust that when you really are ready—scared or not—the Universe will set people and opportunities in your path to help you succeed.

When you commit, you are actually committing to yourself. You are recognizing and honoring your own value and loving yourself in a way that nobody else possibly can. You are making a pledge to stop relying on outside sources—your boss, your spouse, fate, or anything else—to bring you fulfillment. You are laying claim to all that lies within you and recognizing that you are already in possession of everything you need. Commitments become blessings because you have learned to love yourself in a way that now supports the fulfillment of your purpose and the decisiveness that aligns with the life you are committed to creating.

Now here's the fun part! To fully embrace your commitment, you get to overcome a series of traps and pitfalls—the stumbling blocks the shadow creates in order to keep itself alive. Instead of judging your shadow, though, for making your journey difficult, I encourage you to say thank you. Your shadow, after all, has kept you safe and comfortable many times. It just doesn't serve you any longer.

One of the most common traps is what I call the "someday" trap. If you've been telling yourself that "someday" you'll get in shape, or quit your job, or move to your dream city, or start that business, then you haven't really committed to your vision. Sure, you've thought about it, and that's great and all, but . . . in reality you're doing just the opposite: *creating empty promises to yourself that actually stop you from having to commit at all.* New Year's resolutions are a mass example of the "someday" trap. Think about it: If you aren't committed to getting in shape in December, why are you suddenly going to be committed in January? Does the calendar have the magical ability to dictate the course of your life and how you show up? Of course not. If it's something you can put off, then it's something you're not feeling in your cells. It's not a commitment. It's a hope, a dream, a wish—all things that can only be made real when you give up your excuses and commit to the process.

There are other versions of this trap too. Maybe for you it's money—you don't have enough in savings to start your business or join that gym. A deep commitment doesn't mean you'll instantly strike gold, but it will adjust your thinking. You'll find ways to reduce your expenses, to generate more, and to save. Or you'll find ways to get in shape that don't involve a monthly bill—a good set of running shoes, for example, should last you hundreds of miles. Creating that commitment will engage your creativity and observations in ways you never considered and lead to possibilities you never imagined.

I also encourage you to reconsider the way you think of abundance in your life. If you focus constantly on what you don't have, you'll focus entirely on lack—and a mind-set of lack only creates more lack. Instead, if you focus on all the ways in which you are abundant, you'll not only feel better and more grateful in the moment, but you'll create the opposite effect—because abundance creates more abundance. It's all just a matter of focus! So release the helpless mind-set of thinking, *This is all there is.* Because that's only true if you believe it to be.

You Don't "Deserve." You Simply "Are."

I don't use the term *deserve*, because it's a fundamentally flawed concept. The idea that you deserve something suggests you might *not* deserve something else. This creates a sense of lack and disempowerment, a sense that failure is the default state.

Mantra: *I love myself enough to know and believe wholeheartedly that I get to have what I most desire in this life, simply because I'm here on this planet at this time.*

This is not to be confused with an entitlement mentality. You still gotta work for it!

Commitment is activated in a three-step process. The first step is deciding. Take a look at your list of three to five items again and consider your desires for each one. Think about them in terms of not only what you stand to gain but also what you are proposing to give and how the Universe may benefit from your commitment. This will require a little more meditation on your part. For example, if you wrote that one of your desires is to make a certain amount of money, then consider what that truly means in the bigger picture. What would you do with the extra money? Would you use it to give something back? If the answer is yes, the Universe is much more likely to reward your commitment. If the answer is no, then reconsider what you are asking for and why you are asking for it. We all come from Source, so if your desires take that connection into account, you will be much more aligned with the natural workings of the Universe. Now choose one of those desires to focus on.

Once you've decided on your first desire, the next step is to declare it. Say it out loud. Write it down. Tell a friend. This is where that accountability partner can be particularly helpful. When you state your intention to somebody else, it's much harder to back down from it. That's called integrity—and it's something to take seriously. Cast your commitment out into the world, where it can begin to gather energy and start its work. Doesn't that feel great?

The final step is to take action—immediate, meaningful action. The energy of transformation is similar to that of a snowball rolling down a hill. It can develop into an earth-changing avalanche, but without an initial push, an investment of actual movement, nothing happens.

A good place to start taking action is with your *ways of being*—a critical concept in the *You Be You* process. Your ways of being are the qualities that make you who you are; they are how you choose to show up for yourself and others in every moment, in every interaction of your day. Your ways of being are the most fundamental thing you can change—there's no paperwork, no monetary investment, no extra time required. You simply commit to showing up with the energy and vibration equal to the things you want to attract and—voilà! For instance, if your goal is to experience more love in your relationship, then one way of being will be to show up with more love. If your goal is to attract more money, then one way of being will be to demonstrate openness and generosity, remembering that money is frequency, or energy.

So for that all-important first action, commit to changing your ways of being—demonstrate your desires in the very next interaction you have with somebody and in every single one after that. Then watch carefully as the Universe recognizes your investment and rises up to meet you with new possibilities because it wants to see you succeed. It wants to see you fulfill your purpose, have massive heart-expanding experiences, give back, and be ignited by love, all while creating impact by giving of yourself to the world—because guess what? You were created to be exactly *who you are*. Now is your time to come back to that person and celebrate the gift you are to the world.

Exercise: Make It Official

It's time to wrap up your work on commitment with an official declaration to yourself, acknowledging your own powerful light, that you are committed to living as your authentic self, and that you are ready to show up in alignment with your highest desires. Fill out the following:

I, _____ [your name here] commit to

_____

_____

_____

[three to five ways of being] because I love myself so much

that I want _____ [desire] for myself, and I

believe it's possible because I said so.

Signature _____

Date _____

Chapter 2

KNOW YOUR WHYDENTITY

If identity is who you are, then *whydentity* is a deeply considered, authentic version of that. It's the self you build around your true purpose, the way your individual light manifests through your thoughts and actions in this world, and the reason you have the vibrational frequency you do. In the course of my work at Fitlife.tv, I've had the pleasure of helping many of our community members discover and tap into the power of their whydentities. Not only is it one of my favorite things to do with people, it's also a huge component of why we've had so much success in helping people transform their lives.

When people come to us for guidance, we don't settle for the take-two-of-these-and-call-us-in-the-morning approach. We look for the reasons behind our clients' issues—and I'm not talking about the surface-level stuff. Take the case of Diana, who came to us seeking weight loss. She'd tried all the fad diets but none of them had worked, so we started digging, as we do with all our clients. It took a lot of courage for Diana to admit that she was habitually overeating in order to hide the pain of a difficult marriage, but we were just getting started. I prodded her with questions—about her husband, her upbringing, her early childhood—and eventually we got to the true heart of the matter: as a young girl, she'd witnessed conflict and fighting in her parents' marriage, and that had modeled patterns and expectations that had steered her unconsciously to her own marriage. This was our first conversation, and I'll never forget the stunned look on her face as the full realization of the situation dawned on her. It was a huge revelation for her to process, but with it we were able to guide her to a program to not only change her eating but also to address the ongoing challenges she was facing with her husband and her parents.

Maybe the most notable of all these cases for me personally is that of our very own C.E.O., Djamel. Djamel first came to us as a client in the very beginning of Fitlife. tv's creation, seeking physical transformation. He was an aerospace engineer at the time, and a good one. Really good. He was doing what he believed would make his parents proud career-wise, which was important to him. He was making good money and climbing the ranks quickly. At least on the surface, he had achieved some measure of harmony in the success department.

But he wasn't fully happy with his physical being—he felt he was too thin, and he wanted to learn to develop more strength and power in a healthy way. I had him come over to my house one day, along with about a dozen of his friends who had also come to Fitlife.tv to undertake a 90-day transformation that we had developed. The program always began with an intensive conversation about the participants' current realities and the changes they desired, and during the course of this, I pressed Djamel on his *why*. Why was he doing what he was doing as an engineer? Did it really make him happy, or was he doing it for others?

As the conversation got more intense and emotional, Djamel was able to tap into the deeper levels of his role on this planet and how he was showing up, and he discovered that his true desire was to impact lives in a more direct and uplifting manner. (It just so happened that he too loved health and transformation.) While there had been financial reward, social status, and some satisfaction in meeting his family's expectations with his work developing drones and technology for customers like the U.S. Army, none of it aligned with his authentic self, with the place inside him that craved radical inspiration. Furthermore, every time Djamel went to work, he had to walk past a sign that advised him, *Enter at your own risk.* You see, many of the materials Djamel was working with were carcinogenic, and the sign went on to explain that anyone who walked through that door was at risk for the dreaded word: *cancer.* Somehow all those expectations he carried, as well as his professional status and earnings, had trumped his conscious decisions about his health and made it okay for him to walk past that sign every weekday. Deep inside, though, that choice was taking its toll on his mind, body, and spirit and leaving him desiring more fulfillment and purpose in a way that felt safe. And while he couldn't quite put his finger on the specifics yet, somewhere in his being he knew the impact he was having on the world was not completely in line with his real desires. As this realization settled in over the course of our conversation, Djamel's eyes began to fill with tears.

Since then I've learned this was a pivotal moment in guiding him to the path he ultimately chose to follow, which completely transformed his life. Not only did it put him on the course that would lead to us becoming business partners and creating Organifi, our organic superfoods company, it also unlocked other directions for him, like interests in personal development, skydiving, and dance. And it all stemmed from the whydentity process—the search for why you are who you are and ways to align your purpose with how you show up and share your unique gifts each day.

The Why That Makes You Cry

Profound revelations like Djamel's are not uncommon when you're tapping into your true essence—your reason for being here, your purpose on this planet, your heart's greatest calling, your undeniable whydentity. This is the very thing that creates such emotion within you that you know, without a doubt, is exactly *who* you are and *why* you are here in this very moment. This is the *why* that makes you *cry*. It's a full-body experience, as if you're recognizing a long-lost twin. And in a sense you are. You're completing a circle, discovering a part of you that has been buried beneath the muck of impossible expectations. Yes, it's that powerful—and we all have it.

Where does your whydentity come from? I believe it's given to us before we're born, put into every cell in our bodies, as fundamental as DNA. Your authentic purpose is already beginning to work on your decisions as you select your beginning before you even arrive on earth, and one of the big tasks of your lifetime is to tap into that pre-existing purpose. To *remember* it and come back home.

Remember the story I shared in the introduction, about the beginning of my own life? My purpose led me to select that series of trials early in my life because on some level, I believe, I knew it was the pathway that would lead me toward my authentic self. I knew it was a pathway that would serve as a test and a choice—I could choose empowerment or a victim mentality. I'll admit there have been victim moments along the way, but I continue to choose higher, choose better and more truthfully, and those victim moments rarely come along anymore. It didn't happen overnight, but that's where the beauty of the journey lies. And with so much at stake, the choice of empowerment and growth has been something I have committed to fully because I know with every ounce of my being that everything and everyone has a reason in their lives. And in this way, my path is really no different than yours.

This doesn't mean my work was complete at birth, of course! The circumstances of those early years, and all the years after them, for that matter, influenced both my understanding of my purpose and the way I continue to consciously build my whydentity around it. It wasn't always a linear process—there were false starts, there was trial and error, like the errors that led to me being overweight and dissatisfied with my life and my business in Tampa Bay. I'd built my identity around a surface-level *why*—a purpose that aligned with what and who I thought I should be instead of who I really was and now proudly am.

Finding Your True Purpose

Think about your own life. Maybe there are areas that look a lot like "success." Maybe you've got a high-status, high-paying job and a nice house. Maybe you get compliments on your appearance or even on your talents. Does it give you a deep sense of satisfaction, though? Or are you doing everything you're supposed to be doing because that's what society tells you?

I'm guessing there's some doubt in there somewhere—a sense that if things were different, you would actually be happier and more aligned with the authentic you. I'm not talking about simply acquiring more stuff or moving up the ladder society tells you you're supposed to be climbing, but about something much deeper, much more real—a feeling of peace within yourself because your life just feels good. If you do have the sense that you're not quite there yet, it's likely because the reality you are currently living in does not fully support the true version of yourself, the version that lives deep down at your core. And that's okay. No judgments here! This is simply the space to lovingly create awareness of your soul's desires so you can shift in a way that brings you back to your purpose and lets you light the world up with your gifts.

How do you know you have rediscovered (or maybe discovered for the first time) who you are and the reason you were so thoughtfully placed in this life experience, right here, right now? Like Djamel, you'll know with certainty because you will feel it so deeply it'll overwhelm you with emotion. The conviction in your heart will grab hold of you and have you feeling lighter, freer, unstoppable. That is why we say it's the *why that makes you cry*—because, most times, it does exactly that! When that deep sense of commitment we talked about in Chapter 1 comes easily, you will know you have arrived. There is no right time frame either. As long as you are committed and doing the work to figure it all out, then ultimately, the Universe will reward your efforts. But only when you align with it in a way that is true and pure and real.

Remember the story I shared of my realization at the beach next to the crashing waves? It was on that day that I experienced all this for the first time. Remember my moment of commitment, the desire I sent out into the

Universe for $70,000 so I could start a business that would serve my true purpose? Well, alignment and Source came together, and it was only a week after that day that my buddy Preston, who was also in the finance business, called me to ask if I wanted to create a webinar on credit and debt and offer it for maybe a thousand dollars. While I didn't quite grasp the immensity of my *yes* at the time, I agreed to his request and immediately developed a course to promote to his mailing list. I really didn't think much more about it . . . until one morning soon after, when I awoke and checked my bank account and discovered a balance of $67,486. I was shocked! It didn't even dawn on me at first that it had come from the webinar, but there it was—almost exactly what I had asked for.

I took this as a divine sign—the manifestation of the vision I'd cast into the Universe—that I was being rewarded for honoring my clarity and taking radical action. This was exactly what I needed to catapult me to the next step. And then it was time to follow through.

That is the kind of thing I am talking about. When you align with your truth and take action, the Universe wants to support you—and ultimately, if you stay open, you will see signs of this in your daily encounters and experiences. But that's the key: stay open. Detach from how you think it should look and trust that whatever comes your way has a purpose.

You've probably heard that the first step of transformation is to change your environment, and it's true. I realized it was time to remove myself from Tampa and the friends I had made there who no longer felt right for the energy and vibration I was working to share with the world. So I jumped ship and moved to San Diego, where I used my flip cam to start shooting videos about wellness. I did this every day and posted them on YouTube, and almost immediately Fitlife.tv was born. The business exploded—I had no idea how much power sharing myself with the world had until I made the leap and stopped worrying so much about materialistic things and how others viewed me. Here I was, living proof that changing the way we choose to view and live with our stories is totally possible when that change aligns with our truth and is centered around giving instead of getting. And better yet, it's never too late to start. (Do you hear me? I'm talking to you, my friend. It's *never* too late to start. Not for anybody!)

I continued to honor my newfound purpose by studying, reading a book or two a week, juicing green vegetables, and sharing videos about my transformation, and in 90 days I lost those 40 pounds. I felt incredible! My energy was through the roof. I was meeting absolutely amazing people. I finally felt like I was doing exactly what I was placed on this planet to do.

During the process I documented my entire journey and began posting pictures of my progress, despite my initial apprehension about how others might respond. I was floored when stories started coming in from all kinds of people who could relate to my journey. In just six months, I amassed 400,000 followers on social media and was creating a movement that I felt really good about. I'd found my true purpose, rebuilt my identity and a growing brand around it, and committed to doing everything I could to honor it, and the Universe had risen up and met me.

That is the power of taking the time to dig in and figure out your whydentity. It's available to everyone— including you, as you are reading this now! The journey to uncover the truth will look different from person to person, but isn't that the beautiful part? Knowing there is no right or wrong way—there is only *your* way. This should feel empowering and exciting! This alone should create emotion, because it's big . . . huge . . . giant! This one realization literally has the potential to create massive shifts in every single area of your life—if you let it. And if, and only if, you dive in and trust that the net will appear . . . at exactly the right time. Don't worry about *how*—it's none of your business! The Universe will take care of that.

Exercise: Write from the Future

In this exercise you'll practice visualizing the end results of all we've discussed in this chapter: the discovery of your true purpose and the formation of your whydentity. Write a journal entry about yourself five years from now, the version of you who's living completely from your whydentity. Use the following as prompts:

- What changes were you blessed to make?
- What career path are you absolutely dominating? (I see you . . . I know you're a total badass.)
- Are your relationships fulfilling? Loving? Respectful? Aligned with the newfound *you*?
- What new habits have you developed to stay the course and continue moving forward?
- How have your thoughts shifted? Maybe it's as simple as choosing to see things as blessings instead of "have to's."
- Who are you positively impacting daily?
- How are you sharing your gifts?

Once you have completed your entry, I want you to take a picture with your phone and make it your screen saver. Or rip the pages out of your journal and tack them up somewhere you can see them daily. Or do what so many others have done and use this as a basis for creating a vision board with pictures to really *see* the full view of the life you are creating. Whatever method you decide on, make it a daily practice to come back to this vision and align your everyday decisions as best you can. Maybe even set a reminder every two or three days to reread your vision and ask yourself where you can modify it to continue moving closer toward your goals.

Chapter 3

HONOR THE BODY

Although your body is ultimately just a vessel for your spiritual, vibrational self, your body, mind, and spirit are so deeply intertwined that you can't transform one without the other areas shifting to accommodate the whole you. If all the brilliance of your individual light is going to shine through you and out into the world, the practice of developing a harmonious relationship with your body is imperative. Without this very important piece of your transformation, you'll be left feeling out of sorts, or "off," instead of feeling light and free, flowing effortlessly through life. (Remember—this does not mean there won't be challenges. It simply means they will not affect you in the same way if your mind, soul, and body are all working in harmony to support the real you.)

I invite you to take a moment to think about how you feel in your current physical body. Does your physical self align with your soul, with who you truly are? If not, how does this disconnection affect your confidence? How does it affect the way you show up in the world? How does it affect your excitement for trying new things, stretching your comfort zone, taking risks? I don't want this disconnection to hold you back any longer. And I know you don't want it to either. The life you desire and the health you desire are available to you—no matter where you are right now.

The truth is, if you're not treating yourself right, with proper nutrition and exercise and with thoughts and actions that support health, then your body will reflect it. While your physical body is not at all who you are, it is a barometer of truth as to how you show yourself love— or don't. On a cellular level, you are very literally made of the things you eat and more importantly, what you absorb. The way you move and the thoughts you think all play a role in the manifestation of how you show up, in every way.

Your Body: The Foundation for Transformation

Think about your reactions when meeting someone new, or looking in the mirror, or, perhaps most acutely, when you're considering being intimate with someone for the first time. If you're not honoring your body in a way that resonates with your core essence, then each of these moments carry pieces of anxiety and misgiving, blocking your light and keeping you small.

In order to realize the full brilliance of your light, you've got to start making decisions today that will put you on the path toward the physical transformation that will support your mental and spiritual transformation. In fact, I want you to start thinking of yourself as the captain of your body, rather than just a passenger. Or maybe as the C.E.O. As you can imagine, an effective C.E.O. has to make difficult decisions, often sacrificing short-term benefits for the long-term health of their enterprise. To guide their daily decisions, a C.E.O. must constantly return to their mission statement—their company's purpose.

As the C.E.O. of your body, it's no different. Your whydentity is your mission statement, and reminding yourself of this every time you make food choices— coupled with the commitment you made to this process in Chapter 1—will help you overcome the long-established temptations and habits that have been sabotaging your attempts at leveling up and embracing the highest version of yourself. Shift your mind-set so you're making decisions based on your deeper purpose rather than the day's short-term pleasures.

This is what drove me in my own physical transformation. I'm from Michigan, and while I have a deep love for my home state and all its people, it's a place that encouraged some less-than-ideal health habits, for me personally anyway. Gray skies for eight months of the year and a harsh winter meant lots of time indoors, eating comfort foods like pizza, Hamburger Helper, macaroni and cheese, you name it. Those were my go-to meals growing up, and my upbringing with unhealthy comfort foods set me up for a lot of extra weight in my 20s when I was in Tampa. I was a much bigger Canole then!

But when I realized it was my mission and purpose to help others lead healthier lives, I knew that had to start with me. I developed a workout regimen, and each time I headed to the gym, I had a sense that it wasn't just about me and my own body, but a real step in making a difference in a lot of people's lives. When I anchored my workouts to my *why*, everything became intentional, from the type of music I'd choose to the particular muscle groups I focused on to the food I was feeding myself before and after. There were setbacks, of course. I'd make a lot of progress and then I'd slip back into those old comforting habits I'd learned in Michigan. But I never quit. It isn't always comfortable to level up, to embrace your light, but I promise you—the person on the other side of that fear and discomfort has a lot to offer. And I know you're wildly curious about who you are with all the limitations stripped away!

Body, Mind, and Spirit

I continue to focus on the body, both for myself and for the community I am committed to serving, because it's a critical component of how we show up in the world. And also because it's relatively easy to take immediate, concrete steps to honor it. It's a great place to begin developing positive habits that will quickly carry over to your mind and spirit.

What do I mean by this? Think of it this way: When you're new to meditation, it's very common to feel uncertain or even lost. You might come away from your early sessions feeling frustrated or confused, and wondering, *Did I do that right? How is this helping me? How am I supposed to know what changes to make? Did I meditate long enough?* But if you opt for fresh salad at lunch rather than that fast-food meal, you know with 100 percent certainty that you did the right thing. Not only do you know it in your mind, you know it with literally every cell in your body, each of which is going to benefit from your decision. The benefits don't stop there though. Eating healthy will also bring about a better sense of well-being, which ultimately provides more room for your authentic self, and yes, your light. Just that one small, concrete decision can be the beginning of a pattern, where you nurture and honor your authentic being with the determination to make the hard decisions you need to.

This equivalency works the other way also. Just as your nutritional reality can influence your spiritual reality, there is a school of thought that describes how your degree of well-being can also play a role in determining your cravings. For instance, if you're craving sweets, it can be an indicator of an underlying sadness in your life. Chocolate in particular can boost serotonin levels, so a strong craving for it can indicate mood problems. Salt cravings often arise in people who are undergoing too much stress, and fat cravings can be indicators of emotional pain and loss or feelings of low self-worth.

I had a friend, Nancy, who used to "need" something sweet after each meal (even breakfast!). And no matter how she changed her diet, that craving never subsided. It wasn't until she dug into the missing spiritual component of her whydentity that Nancy felt truly satisfied after her meals, dropping the "need" for sweets and even dropping a few pounds in the process. So often what we really crave is a connection to something we may not even know we are lacking, whether emotional, spiritual, or something else altogether. We crave what we crave due to lack *somewhere* in our lives. As a society we have been so conditioned to fill these voids with food, it's no wonder we live in the most overfed nation, with obesity rates and health issues skyrocketing, even in young children. When we get honest about the reasons we crave what we crave, it's that much easier to find solutions that fill us up the *right* way and allow us to flourish and thrive in the body we were so blessed with.

Once you embrace yourself in mind, body, and spirit and recognize your own importance, what you'll crave the most is a return to your authentic self—which means thinking of food not merely as food but as energy. So ask yourself what sort of energy brings out your best self.

For some this means plant-based nutrition, but others will find that poultry or red meat sustains their highest vibrations. Everyone is unique, and a clear connection to your intuition (much more on this later!) will help you determine what's best for you. Once you are guided by your intuitive understanding of what your body wants, you'll make better decisions about your energy sources. This will bring your body, mind, and spirit into harmony, increasing your ability to make an impact and to show up for people as a higher version of yourself.

Mental Juicing

For me it all began with a single glass of green juice. I was at work one day and my buddy brought in what looked like a cup of swamp water. He could tell I needed it—he could see my tiredness in the way I carried myself and in my eyes. I didn't cave without a fight though. The idea of chugging this glass of green gunk was far from appealing. But I was at a pivotal point, and on some level I knew I needed to do something. As it turned out, this push came at the right time. I drank the juice, and when all those pure nutrients worked their way into my cells, I was amazed at how good I felt. It really was almost immediately that I felt a sense of clarity and stamina. That decision to embrace the unknown and try something new sent me down a path that would very literally change my thought patterns and make me understand the importance of tapping into my deeper purpose and moving fully into my whydentity. That one small step triggered a transformation I am still living and loving and sharing, all over the world, every day.

If you have been watching our channel over the years, you probably know that I'm a huge proponent of the transformative powers of vegetables and juicing. Not only did juicing fuel my own journey, but I've seen it work on thousands of others as well. The key to it all is the incredible ability of plants to create nutrients.

We all know the sun, that gorgeous, vibrant, ball of heat and light, is the source of all life here on earth. And short of gobbling up photons directly, eating fruits and vegetables is our most direct connection to that extraordinary source of energy. When I take a sip of juice, I think of it as liquid light, which is in a sense exactly what it is. Thanks to the unique powers of photosynthesis, the sun's photons have undergone just one simple transformation in order to become pure nutrition for the human body, and the high vibrations of those fruits and vegetables (preferably organic!) are the best possible fuel for our incredibly intelligent bodies.

The benefits of feeding your body such a pure source of nutrients reach through your whole emotional, energetic, and physical being. On a biological level, science has long been acquainted with the power of fruits and vegetables and their micronutrients to fight cancer and to fight the effects of aging on our chromosomes, and now we are learning more and more about probiotics and the gut biome, which is completely integral to our overall well-being.

On a mental level, a healthier, happier body means your mind will be lighter, freer, and less encumbered in the endless cycle of craving, guilt, and regret that comes with the habitual eating of unhealthy, processed food. When your cells and muscles are getting all the vitamins and minerals they need, your mind no longer has to devote resources to survival and is free to focus on emotions and other higher functions. Your body will have the proper bio constituents to formulate the neurotransmitters necessary for proper neurological functioning and mental health. You'll be thriving, not just surviving.

And on a spiritual level, you'll be more in harmony with nature, knowing you're not contributing to the harmful practices so prevalent in commercial farming and ranching. You can enhance this knowledge by taking a moment to be grateful for the food and water you have. It's easy to take it all for granted, but it's important to remember to be thankful. With each meal notice as many positive things as possible—everything from your good fortune to have access to fresh, clean water to the color of a bright green vegetable to the scent and texture and taste of a fresh peach. This practice will help your spirit derive the full benefit of the nutrition you're choosing.

All this means more clarity throughout all levels of your being, and more clarity means fewer obstructions standing between the powerful vibrations of your authentic being and all the ways you could be showing up in the world.

The Three-Day Body Preparation

Now, chances are if you are familiar at all with our movement at Fitlife.tv, you have heard me speak openly and passionately about fueling the body with whole foods and copious amounts of green juice. And if you're new to our mission, you're about to get a dose of one of the most powerful tools we use to create transformation, which is resetting the body to allow for maximum absorption of quality nutrients, which in turn creates massive internal reprogramming and sets you up for success from the inside out!

I am not going to complicate this. In fact, I am going to keep this super simple because I want you to get used to using the tools available to you without any room for excuses. I know those excuses can creep in—I've been there too! But with this incredibly easy-to-follow three-day protocol, excuses won't even stand a chance! Seriously, it's that easy, but it'll take your commitment, so let's make it official. Ready?

Day 1: Upon waking, drink one cup of warm lemon water. I've got options for you, from beginner to advanced, so choose what works for you!

- **Beginner:** Squeeze the juice of 1/2 to 1 whole lemon into a glass of warm water. Add 1 to 2 teaspoons of raw honey and a dash of cinnamon.

- **Intermediate:** Follow the same steps as the beginner option and add 1 tablespoon raw apple cider vinegar (with the "mother" included—you will see this labeled on the bottle, like in my favorite brand, Bragg).

- **Advanced:** Eliminate the raw honey and increase the apple cider vinegar to 2 tablespoons. I like to add a pinch of cayenne pepper too, to clear out my sinuses!

Do this every morning of the three-day protocol, creating a consistent habit. This does some incredible things inside your body, from flushing the liver of toxins to revving up your metabolism to clearing your skin and boosting your immunity.

Day 2: Add a nutrient-dense green juice for your mid-morning snack. Most people who are new to juicing tend to do a 50:50 fruit to veggies ratio. As your palette changes and you begin to free yourself from those awful sugar cravings, your body will crave more veggies (funny how that happens). The goal is ultimately to go "full veg," or in simpler terms, to get as many quality, low-glycemic veggies in your juice as possible while eliminating most of the fruit. This may be easy for you if you've been juicing for a while already or have already adopted a more alkaline diet. If not, that's totally okay. A juice with a 50:50 ratio is still a great first step. One of the biggest reasons we created Organifi was to give people a simple solution and eliminate the excuses that juicing is too time-consuming, confusing, messy, etc. So our juice products are always an option if you're looking for something balanced and convenient. Bottom line: it's time to get your juicing game on point and give your cells some love!

Day 3: Now you have a morning and midmorning ritual in the works, so on Day 3 your goal is to swap a heavy meal with a salad. This will keep the momentum going as you shift to cleaner fuels to nourish your cells at the deepest level and support your digestion in the process. Healthy digestion will result in more balanced moods (because 80 to 90 percent of your serotonin—the happy hormone—is housed in your gut!); clearer, more vibrant skin; better immunity; regular bowel movements; less bloating; and an overall better state of being!

So there it is! In three days you have implemented three new upgrades and have begun forming habits to fuel your journey from within. The goal now is to keep it going, using these three simple tips each day to bring you that much closer to the elevated human who is just begging to emerge and join forces with other light-bringers!

Exercise: The "Before" Picture

Take a photograph of yourself now—before you begin your three-day body preparation, before embarking on the remainder of this book's program. Make sure your eyes are showing! You can see so much when you look into someone's eyes. A reminder—you are absolutely not allowed to judge yourself. Instead, I want you to intentionally take this picture, with however much hope and possibility you hold in your heart, honoring the space you are in now, giving gratitude to your body for the journey it has been on and where it is yet to go.

PART II

Crush Your Limitations

Part I was all about preparation. You prepared your body by examining and changing the way you feed it. You prepared your mind as you better understood the power of commitment and you created a contract to hold yourself accountable for your own commitment. You prepared your spirit by meditating on your deeper purpose and rebuilding your whydentity around your authentic self. Chances are some of this felt a little uncomfortable. You may have felt scared as you dove into all of this and got real with yourself. That's totally normal! A big hug to you for making it through. And while this is only the beginning, I want to congratulate you on what you have done so far. I'm proud of you.

Now it's time to get messy. You knew that was coming, didn't you? Of course! Because this, my friend, is where the real magic happens. Part II of the journey is the plunge into the heart of the forest. It's the darkest part of the journey. If you're Bilbo Baggins, it's when you run up against Smaug, the dragon of unspeakable power. Or if you're Luke Skywalker, it's when you discover your friends have been captured by the bad guy, who is really your dad, and then you get your hand chopped off. If you are on a quest for personal transformation—and if you're reading this then I know you are—it's when you take a close, hard look at every last thing that's holding you back and make the tough decisions that will either send you down a pathway toward the sunny clearings on the far edge of the forest or lead you back into the old habits that were keeping you in the dark.

Chapter 4 is about diving into the mess. It's about how to keep going when things start to get hard. It's about transforming buried trauma and hidden emotions and turning them into rocket fuel. In Chapter 5 you'll face your fears head-on. We'll run through a list of specific fears—even fear of death—and study what's at their roots and how you can break free of their limitations. Chapter 6 will walk you through a process for identifying your limitations and discovering why they're in place. You'll learn from the real-world examples of people who've been conditioned to hold limiting beliefs but have identified and overcome them.

Trust me when I say I have been down this path myself and have had the absolute honor of helping millions of others find their way down, through, and *out* as well. You are not alone. The steps I'll provide over the next three chapters will bring you through that darkness, allowing you to rise up and step into the you that has been there all along—the you that will finally be free to shine.

Chapter 4

DIVE INTO
THE MESS

By this point in the journey, you've prepared yourself inside and out and you've gotten a handle on some of the things in your life that are not authentically you. You've envisioned a brighter future, made plans for concrete action, and taken the first steps. If you're like most people, you'll find that initial excitement beginning to wear off. The end goals seem miles away and the effort to get yourself there seems overwhelming. There are voices in your head telling you it's too hard, that you don't really need to do all of this anyway, that things weren't *really* all that bad before. And besides, what if you're going the wrong way? Or what if nothing changes?

You're questioning everything about your journey—your motivation, your desires, even the value of your true, soul-defining purpose. You find yourself wanting to turn around and go back to being your old self, because let's face it, that was much simpler and you already knew the outcome (even if it didn't make you happy). In short: everything's a mess.

Well, welcome to the middle of the journey. Yes, it probably feels hard, and probably pretty messy. These feelings you're experiencing are (1) real, (2) valid, and (3) perfect! Because if life were easy and comfortable, you would already *be* in the place you desire, right? You wouldn't be in this mess in looking for a shovel to dig your way out! But you are, and that's okay. So stick with me . . . let's do the work together.

I've got news for you, Grasshopper. And I want you to listen closely. This process doesn't have to be what you would typically consider "hard." Instead, I encourage you to look at it as a blessing, because it is. And I want you to give Source, the Universe, God, whomever, some hearty thanks! 'Cause guess what? Everything you need to get yourself through this stage of the journey is already inside you. Now, before you go shaking your head, hear me out and really feel the words laid out on the pages in front of you.

Within you lies compassion, which is one of your most fundamental abilities, one that will allow your transformation to unfold and that will support your success. If you can tap into your compassion and self-love, you'll discover the very important truth that we are *all* messy. We all have a shadow. And I am going to teach you how to love this part of yourself, just as you love your light. They need each other, after all. You wouldn't see the vibrancy of the stars without the sun setting to create darkness, right? The same goes for the human form that is you. This part of the journey is dark and at times may seem more difficult than other parts. This is true for everybody who's willing to embark on a journey of change in order to be free.

I learned my own lessons in self-compassion when I finally realized it was time to face my childhood traumas head-on. I'd done such a careful job of packing them up and locking them in a closet in my mind. I'd been able to fool myself into believing if I just pretended they didn't exist, I could achieve success and happiness without confronting them. And with money, friends, and a successful business, there wasn't much to make me believe otherwise. (At the time I was pretty good at ignoring the now-obvious lack of fulfillment and the uncomfortable, unhealthy excess weight!) But deep inside my soul, my trauma was gradually affecting everything else, creating shadows where there once was light. And then one day, it all caught up with me, and I realized I couldn't wait any longer—it was time to face my past. I had to open that closet up again and remove everything I had so carefully and meticulously put away in their little boxes, including all the pain and broken dreams. By then—with the help of my mentor, Frank, and with a deeper understanding of my true purpose—I was in a place on my own journey where I was able to view everything I'd been hiding with compassion. I was able to send my past experiences so much love and light that I could shift the entire vibration around them and see them for what they really were: *lessons*. I can't say I got rid of the trauma—I don't think you can ever get rid of stories like that. But with compassion for myself and my past, I was able to transform it for good, so it could generate positive energy and momentum to fuel my purpose of helping others transform their lives, rather than keeping me stuck in the darkness.

It's okay to feel doubt, discouragement, frustration, and all those emotions that make you want to turn back and give up. It's perfectly natural. In fact, it means you're on the right path. But if you want to get to the other side of the transformation process, you've got to cultivate the habit of shifting. This means accepting the former state of things and making the conscious decision to choose better in order to empower yourself to move forward despite frustration and doubt.

If you're having trouble finding compassion for yourself at this stage of the journey, try this experiment. Imagine calling up Jesus, Buddha, God, the mind of the Universe, or whatever transcended entity or masters you most closely connect with. Imagine sitting next to them—perhaps on a hillside, looking out over a beautiful meadow on a sunlit afternoon—and sharing your story and your journey with them. What would they tell you? Would they judge you, scorn you, or tell you it's hopeless and you should turn back? The very suggestion of that is ridiculous, right? They would treat you and your story with infinite compassion, and they would not let you walk away from that meeting without making sure you knew the endless extent of your abilities, your potential, your strength. They would destroy even the slightest hint of judgment with their unrelenting love and continuous compassion. You are not separate from them—you are them, just as they are you—so now is the time to practice this same type of comforting embrace as you wrap your heart and soul around your truth and allow yourself space to spread those beautiful wings and fly. There's a lot of living left to do, and you have it in you to soar!

Go ahead . . . tap into that sense, that acceptance, to help you confront your darkness. Withhold all judgment, and instead accept your very human reaction to this stage of the journey. Treat yourself with the divine compassion that comes from the belief in a greater sense of your light and your purpose. There's a way through, and you and I will find it together!

Make Your Mess Your Mission

Think for a moment about how we find gold. This precious and beautiful substance is often discovered in some of the most inhospitable environments on earth—deep underground, underwater, in remote areas that are often very cold or very hot. And when we do find our way to the places where it's formed, it's often in tiny pieces, buried in mud.

The gold that lies inside you is similar—you're not going to find it if you're unwilling to get your hands dirty! You've got to stir up all that dirt and mud and open space for the light to shine in so you can see those yellow flecks of glorious gold. Hold on to that thought and make it your mission at this stage to get comfortable being uncomfortable, slide on into the junk, and face what you're up against head-on.

My own mess became my mission about seven years ago. I wasn't making decisions from a place of self-love at the time—instead I was engaged in heavy bouts of escapism, which for me meant drinking on the weekends and feeding my body all the familiar foods I'd learned to comfort myself with back in Michigan: pizza, pasta, macaroni and cheese, chips, you name it. This was the manifestation of my mess. My biological father had tortured me, so here I was decades later as the incarnation of him now torturing myself. I was making the decision every day to eat things that were not contributing to my highest good. Aside from my physical size, my spirit was heavy. I was drowning in a sea of self-preservation. My past had finally caught up to me.

That all changed with my first green juice. Although I was hesitant, I knew the simple act of drinking this one juice was a necessary step, because I could not take for another second the way I was living—playing small and harboring my gifts selfishly instead of allowing myself to step into my authenticity and create something better. I decided in that moment that this juice was the starting point to the rest of my life. That was the permission I was subconsciously seeking to start over, this time with intention and real purpose.

As I continued down that path, making choices that aligned with my desire to be free and of service to the greater good, I had a face-slapping epiphany that my mess wasn't about just what I was putting in my body, but also what I was putting in my mind. I felt a deep, overwhelming desire to work on learning to love and accept myself— the light *and* the dark. Furthermore, I couldn't help but want to help other people, to take all the people I loved and carry them forward with me down that path.

Of course, I still had a lot of work to do to sift through the years of repressed trauma and to face all the darkness that had built up inside me. But once I discovered a pathway forward, empowered by my newfound commitment and enthusiasm, I knew I had the energy and strength to confront everything that was necessary in order to find my way to the other side.

Getting Unstuck

Before we go too much deeper, I want to hone in on one particular aspect of the journey and warn you about a common pitfall that traps many people at this stage: wallowing. Yes, you've got to get yourself all the way up to your neck in that mess. Yes, feeling is a good thing, and you've got to let yourself feel it all in order to heal it all.

Yes, having awareness of your pain can be a powerful tool to move you toward freedom. But there's such a thing as too much.

I've seen it happen many times—people undertake thorough preparations and dive in headfirst, but then they find themselves unable to re-emerge. Once they stir up all those memories and emotions, they get overwhelmed and they replay their original traumas over and over, which not only magnifies the original pain but also creates new pain and oftentimes judgment and anger toward themselves for continuously feeling this way. The result can be a difficult cycle with the opposite result of the intended goal. Rather than being processed and discarded, all that pain grows, leaving very little room for healing to occur.

The issue isn't the feeling of pain in and of itself; it's getting stuck and staying stuck in the pattern of victimhood that blocks healing. Make sense? So I like to suggest time limits. Set a conscious intention to immerse yourself in whatever it is you need to work through, but set a time to emerge from it. Maybe you're in there for five minutes, maybe an hour. Keep it as short as you can while staying true to what you need to do in order to process the emotions and get to the other side.

This doesn't mean your traumas won't come up again—they will. You will almost certainly have to repeat these feeling sessions many times before the pain diminishes enough for you to move through it. What this *does* mean is that you are taking control of the pain in a way that is empowering, authentic, and vulnerable while still acknowledging the work yet to be done. It's a process, but one that warrants your compassionate attention and care, just as you would provide for a friend or loved one.

Trauma as Fuel

Of course, moving from mess to mission isn't the same process for everyone. As unique beings we carry within us our individual stories and personal coping mechanisms, which grow and evolve with us. Your mess may seem big or it may seem small. Either way it's yours to travel through into the light, releasing the things that have kept you heavy throughout the years. You might be the survivor of serious traumas that you haven't been able to face or process yet. If that's the case, you're likely arriving at this stage of the journey feeling more than a little intimidated. And that's okay.

That trauma, that deep layer of black mud? Think of it as untapped potential. If you can approach it with openness, a strong commitment to do the work, and fierce compassion, you'll be able to transform it into pure energy to move you forward into a life far more than you could possibly imagine. I am reminded of this truth daily by Sheree, one of my amazing partners at Fitlife.tv and Organifi.

I met Sheree at the gym years ago and instantly knew we were going to be fast friends. At the time she was working as a holistic health coach, helping people on their path of healing from autoimmune disease, as well as doing women's empowerment coaching, primarily around limiting beliefs and lack of self-worth. Of course, like most of us, she didn't stumble upon her life's work without having her own personal experience to align her to it.

Sheree was open from the beginning about her journey, and what astounded me was how grounded she was in her experience. There was so much I could relate to in her story, and I was inspired by the way she shared so vulnerably, with such conviction. Like me, Sheree is a seeker and believes that everything on our path has a purpose, even the pain. She shared with me that she had grown up with a single mother and had never met her father. She was surrounded by incredibly strong women, which continually reminded her of her own power to create anything she wanted in her life. When she was 18, she left her home in Seattle to move to San Diego for college and to pursue her dreams of working as a stylist for TV and film. It was only a year later that her life completely shifted from the vision she had built up in her mind to something far different, all because of one incident that she eventually chose to see as a gift.

She shared that at the age of 19, she'd been raped. She couldn't believe this had happened to her. And despite being outgoing and outspoken in all other areas of her life, this time she stayed silent—for four years. Yet here she was, a survivor, a title she now wore proudly. And as she shared her experience with me, I couldn't help but wonder what had given her the drive to move through her pain so gracefully. And you know what she told me? *Purpose.* This experience took her from a dream of working in TV and film to a completely different path—a path far more rewarding to her spirit and what she calls her "biggest blessing."

But holding in the pain for all those years created disease in her body, which she dealt with for another nine years. In the process she became her own guinea pig, and eventually she went back to school to study holistic health in order to heal herself and help others do the same. She was determined to get better and share her experiences with abuse and illness openly, because she believed all of it had happened for a reason—the Universe had delivered her true purpose to her, painful as it may have been.

Sheree and I wrote our first book together in 2014, all about autoimmune disease, and since then she's been a huge part in our mission and movement at Fitlife.tv and Organifi. Over the years we've worked on many projects together as she has helped us build our content department. We've written side by side many, many times, from videos to books, and every time we connect, I am reminded of my own strength. She's my mirror, just as I am yours right now, and I feel really good about how far I've come. I'm also really proud of her journey as well.

Can you relate to this? Maybe you have not been through abuse or pain like mine or hers, but possibly you've gone through something that has felt so utterly terrible that all you can think is *Why?* I know I have had moments of questioning over the years, and I used to feel so much shame for the way I judged myself. It took a long time before I could honestly say I was grateful for the struggle. Like Sheree, my pain is where I found my purpose. That shift in mind-set is the most powerful tool I used in my own transformation to get out of my own way and back into my life. And I know it will help you too, if you commit and practice this shift daily. Don't worry if it doesn't come naturally at first. It may not. Instead, focus on how you want to feel and remember that you are in charge of that. It starts in the mind, and everything else will follow.

Exercise: Create Your Self-Love Statement

First, I want to be super clear that should you need permission to feel, here it is! Emotions are one of the greatest gifts we possess, and so often we pass judgment on ourselves for—*gasp!*—not having it all together. Guess what? *You are human!* So if this process feels gross, great. If it brings tears, perfect. If it causes a swirl of chaos in your seemingly picture-perfect environment, *dig in.* Because here you are. And if you truly want to get to the place that will create the most joy and peace in your life, now is the time to embrace the pieces that have led you to this very place. Lovingly thank them for the role they've played and send those that no longer serve you on their merry little way.

Now that you are vibin' with your emotional self, it's time to get real and acknowledge the mess in a new way. On paper, list three to five words or phrases that describe any negative emotions that are coming up for you right now. Here's one example: *I am so overwhelmed; I can't possibly do this.* Or you might simply write, *Overwhelmed.*

Now I want you to rewrite your list, shifting your wording around these feelings to words or phrases that feel empowering! So the previous statement might shift to: *I am grateful for the abundance of growth in front of me, and I am excited to get to the other side of it.*

You can't tell me that didn't feel good! This is a tool you can use in any moment to retrain your brain to cultivate and realize your highest potential. I use this all the time for myself and it's the stepping stone many of my clients have used to release the patterns that keep them stuck, weighed down, and paralyzed in the mess.

Sure, it's simple. But that's the point! Healing doesn't have to be *hard* all the time. The choice is yours, whether you use the tools at your fingertips to keep the training moving (even if it feels really scary and challenging) or choose a path that feels a little less daunting, knowing darn well it will lead you back to the very spot you're sitting in right now.

Chapter 5

FACE YOUR FEARS HEAD-ON

It's time now to turn over the biggest rocks, to shine the light into the farthest corners of the closet and face all that's lurking there. This is the hardest part of the journey, my friend. It's the point when you'll likely find yourself wanting to turn back, because now is the moment when you get to drop all the excuses and dig up the truth about what has *really* been holding you back. It's time to take an honest look at all that has occurred in your life up to this point and, without judgment, dredge up all your worst fears and biggest insecurities. It's time to face the impact they've had on your life and be willing to say goodbye to the pieces that no longer serve the outcome you're committed to creating in your life.

My own journey brought me to this stage back in Tampa, when I came to the realization that almost nothing about my life—my work, my relationships, my surroundings—was in alignment with my deeper purpose. I saw with absolute clarity that I was going to have to leave it all behind, and though I had complete faith in the future, it still meant giving up every bit of stability I'd created up to that point. And remember, for me, stability was a pretty huge deal. I'd suffered horrible abuses as a young boy, and I'd known a lot of financial insecurity, and at that time in my life I had money and what seemed like good friendships. But once I saw that I had to change it all, I knew I had no choice but to face those fears again, and fight through them, in a big way. My journey would take me to San Diego, where I had no income, no home, no family, no friends. It would leave me, once again, to start over alone. I've been through it, and now I'm fortunate to be here to help you through it.

Before we go on, take a moment for reflection. Remember the commitment you made in Chapter 1? Go back to it and remind yourself of the mind-set you were in when you made it—the very reason (your *why!*) that taking this step toward freedom is so important for you. Allow that sense to fill your entire being.

Remember the work you did to create your whydentity? Remind yourself of that deeper purpose and reconnect with your determination to fully express it. Remember the decisions you made about nourishing your body with the right foods to fully support this transformation of your mind and spirit? You might even want to pause here and grab yourself a green juice before continuing. Finally, tap back into that sense of compassion for yourself that you worked so hard to cultivate in the previous chapter. Take your time; breathe deeply; even create a mantra for yourself if you'd like—whatever you have to do to completely hold the knowledge in every one of your cells that your preparations are complete, your commitment is total, and your compassion and overflowing love for yourself is endless. When you're ready, read on. And remember, I'm with you every step of the way as we take this journey into fear.

What Is Fear?

What do you think of when you hear the word *fear*? Perhaps you think of childhood fears, like fear of the dark, or fear of the boogeyman, fear of those strange sounds you heard in the night. Maybe the word *fear* brings up images from scary movies. Maybe it reminds you of the face of a person who left you feeling helpless and afraid. Each of us encounters small fears all the time. Social anxieties, financial insecurities, and all manner of uncomfortable uncertainties permeate our daily lives. Some feel scarier than others, but the truth is, your fears are yours and only you can overcome them. Doing so requires you to reprogram your brain to think of fear in a different way, something that empowers you instead of creating paralyzing thoughts or inaction. I like to think that fear is actually an opportunity. Zig Ziglar says *FEAR* stands for *False Evidence Appearing Real*. Another take on that idea is this inspirational quote (often attributed to Ziglar): "F-E-A-R has two meanings: 'Forget Everything and Run' or 'Face Everything and Rise.' The choice is yours."

The second one feels better, right? So the next time you find yourself in a fear response, think of it instead as a reminder of your innate ability to prosper in the face of adversity. Face whatever is coming up head-on and make the conscious choice to do whatever is necessary to rise anyway.

Common Fear #1: Fear of Your Own Light

This one can feel a little counterintuitive—why would someone be afraid of their own light? Well, embracing your own light means taking full responsibility for your life. It means no more playing the victim, no more blaming others or your upbringing or society or your schedule. It means no more putting things off, no more hiding. It means being vulnerable—showing up in the world as you really, truly are, and sharing your authentic and powerful gifts, even when others may not like it.

Think about this for a moment. If you keep your light locked away, if you keep your authentic self hidden, that feels comfortable and safe. Your authentic self is protected from rejection, from judgment by those who do not or will not connect with your vibration, for reasons of their own. (Note: other people's reactions to you are never actually about you.) The problem with this strategy, of course, is that you're not living in authenticity. You're living an artificial life, pretending to be someone you're not, with the mistaken belief that your true self can flourish while locked inside you. And guess what this creates? An inauthentic outcome that does not align with your *why*, your purpose.

I'm reminded of the story of Bonnie, who was afraid of success because she didn't want to make more money than her husband. And this really isn't all that uncommon, at least in my experience. By society's standards, the generations before us seemed to have stricter beliefs about gender roles. I'm not saying this is good or bad, right or wrong. But for many women I have spoken with, there seems to be an either/or mentality instead of a both/and mentality. Many of them feel they have to choose between being successful in the business world and being successful at home, and for women who value both, as many do, this can be a painful belief to carry. So helping Bonnie understand what was possible for her took some digging—right into her belief patterns and how they came about in the first place.

I had a tough conversation with Bonnie before we spoke to her husband, John. I wanted her to be able to be open and feel confident in her communication with John about how she was feeling. We discussed her childhood programming and the very specific roles each of her parents played in her household. We discussed whether or not she actually shared those beliefs or if she had simply adopted them based on her exposure. We talked about what she wanted to change moving forward to feel more aligned with her spirit and her purpose. I asked her the following questions, as I do with all of my clients, which allowed her to reflect on her current situation without guilt or shame. (This is a great time for you to grab a piece of paper and a pen if any of Bonnie's story resonates with you so far. Take a moment to answer the following questions for yourself and see what comes up.)

The first few questions I asked her were:

1. What did you like about the roles your parents played in your life?
2. How did those positive aspects shape your current reality?
3. Looking back, what do you wish had been different?

Next, I asked her to step back into the present and consider the same series of questions I'd just asked, but in the context of her current relationship with John.

1. What do you like about the roles you and John play in your relationship?
2. How do those positive aspects shape your current reality?
3. What do you wish were different?

The answers were eye-opening, and Bonnie began to cry. The truth was, she'd been judging herself as weak, based on the reality she had learned to create as a small child. She had carried pieces of that with her—as we all do—and they had greatly shaped her beliefs about what she "should" be as a wife and mother. After going through this exercise, she had a better understanding of how her past programming was affecting her beliefs about her relationship with John. This was the missing link to her confidence.

Bonnie had been afraid to make more money than John because she didn't want him to feel like "less of a man," simply put, or like she didn't need him anymore. These feelings were real and valid, and now she was able to share them in a way that felt empowering instead of shaming. I encouraged her to make some time to share this with her husband and to be okay with her fears, to embrace all her emotions. Doing so would allow John to feel safe to do the same, and together they could make a decision that felt good for both of them.

When Bonnie sat down with John, she expressed her fears and explained that when she was growing up, her father had made comments constantly about it being the man's job to provide and take care of the household. He'd always said this with such pride, and her mother seemed to agree wholeheartedly. When she would tell her parents about her dreams of holding a good job like her dad's, they would both assure her that her husband would do that, and that she should worry more about taking care of the home. This felt strange for her, because deep down she wanted more, but she didn't know any different. And all her friends growing up were being taught the same story.

John held her and smiled, thanking her for her vulnerability. They discussed the opportunity she had in front of her and her desire to grow, and John was incredibly supportive. Bonnie went for the promotion—and guess what? She got it! Today Bonnie is thriving in both her personal life and her professional life because she chose to face her fears and to say yes to herself.

Does any of this sound like you? Do you feel like being "successful" will push people away or change things with those you love? The truth is, success looks different for everyone, and people react to change on all sorts of levels. But these are not reasons for you to dim your light.

The opportunity to evolve by following your heart and allowing it to lead you to the places that scare you is a gift. *You* are a gift. So the next time you find yourself doubting your ability to create more success in any area of your life, I want you to think of Bonnie. Because in the end, we all have pieces of Bonnie and John's story in our own reality, and it's up to us—I'm talking to you here!— to take the actions necessary to get to the place where our hearts and souls truly feel free and alive.

It's important to note that there will be times when the person or people you decide to open up to just won't understand. Despite your best efforts, nothing can shield you entirely from the judgments of others—and that's okay! There are a lot of people out there who don't know how to lift themselves up, so they put others down instead. (Maybe this has even been you in the past! If so, acknowledge it, and then give yourself a pat on the back, because that all stops now. You are proof that circumstances and people can change if they choose to.) Detractors will always be out there, and the more you start to live your authentic life, the greater a role you'll play in the world. With this responsibility and honor to be a catalyst for transformation and for what's possible, you're apt to come across even more of them. Instead of putting energy toward those who can't or won't support your expression of your true self, think about how you can increase your vibration to include more love and instead inspire them to step into their own greatness.

It won't always work, though, so when you find that others just don't vibe with your vibe, they ain't yo' tribe! There are billions of people on this planet, and you can't please them all. Some will have a completely different frequency than you, so when you're faced with all different kinds of people, accept that you may be speaking an entirely different language—which, in a spiritual sense, you are—and show them love and kindness anyway. For every one of them, you'll attract a hundred others whose vibration is the same is yours, who are drawn to you precisely because of how clearly and brilliantly you're showing up in the world as yourself.

The potential here for positive, uplifting connections is unlimited—because when you start drawing forth authentic relationships, you become part of something much greater, a web of people who are all committed to supporting one another, who've all chosen vulnerability and positivity over hiding and playing the victim. It's time to stop fearing your own light and *embrace* it—let your light shine! That light of yours is the very thing that can pave the way for so many others to do the same. Whether you know it or not, you can subconsciously grant permission to those who need a sign that it's okay to be exactly who they are. The vulnerability and responsibility that come with embracing your light may take a little getting used to, but once you do, your being and purpose will expand infinitely.

Common Fear #2: Fear of Change

Fear of change is one of the most pervasive fears. We're all affected by it on some level, because we all face periods of uncertainty. It's just part of having a human experience. In fact, nothing in life is permanent. Jobs change, relationships evolve or dissolve, home life fluctuates—each piece of our experience has the potential to shift at any moment, and it's up to us to adapt. It's important to remember that even positive changes can bring about stress and fear. Take, for instance, the upcoming birth of a long-hoped-for child. Amid the joy and excitement, there is bound to be some fear, some anxiety for the way life as you know it is about to change.

Why do we fear change? It comes down to the unknown, and our comfort zones, and our old misguided habit of trying to protect ourselves by keeping ourselves small and our light dim. Once we settle into a certain life, we unconsciously draw a circle around ourselves. This keeps us safe and comfortable. Inside that circle is our everyday life and the things we know we can deal with automatically. Sure, there may be unexpected stressors that arise, but we minimize the chances (or at least we think we do!) that something big will come along and take us by surprise. Outside that circle, things are a little less predictable. We tell ourselves, even if subconsciously, that everything outside our safety circle could possibly be a threat, so we protect ourselves from potential uncertainty and discomfort by playing it safe and sticking to what and who we know. That circle is an illusion though. Life doesn't cooperate with it, and before long your car is breaking down in an unfamiliar neighborhood, or your boss transfers you to a different state, or the doctor tells you you've got a life-threatening disease.

In the early months of my journey with Fitlife.tv, a guy named Nate hired me for coaching. Nate wanted to change, but he didn't quite know how to—he'd simply never learned. He was trying everything he knew to do, but he kept hitting walls. I could tell in our very first meeting that he was determined and ready to realize his own transformation. As we talked we discovered together what might be holding him back: subconscious fear of change.

For some the idea of change can feel exciting. For others though, it can feel downright terrifying. Nate was somewhere in between, so we started to work on strategies he could use to get through his fear. First we needed to better understand where it was coming from. As with Bonnie, I asked Nate three questions that aligned directly with his current situation:

1. When you think of changing your life, what excites you most?

2. Why is it important to you to change in the first place?

3. What does the *new* Nate look and feel like?

It took a bit of back and forth, and it took Nate really digging in and getting a bit uncomfortable with the realization that he was in his own way. His fears of leaving his friends behind, stepping into the unknown, possibly losing everything in the process, not being good enough, not being able to make it financially—these had all become not only excuses but also roadblocks. Without letting go of the excuses and facing these fears head-on, Nate would never be able to get to the place he wanted. Painting a picture of what was possible on the other side of his fears was something Nate hadn't done before, and it was powerful. By taking a good hard look at the life he desired and coming to terms with the role he was playing in each aspect of his journey, he was able to release the limiting beliefs he had been conditioned with over the years: *I'll never be good enough. There is no way I can have it all. Life is just meant to be harder for me.* By acknowledging these limitations and recognizing just how much they were holding him back, he was able to create a new mind-set and rewire his brain with an *I can do anything* attitude. Of course, doing the work was the next step, but changing his patterns internally made a huge difference in the way he showed up, which created a completely different set of outcomes in who and what he was attracting into his life.

I am happy to say that the last time I heard from Nate, he was down 30 pounds, had more energy, was excelling at work, and had renewed his vows with his wife, Karla. He stayed the course, trusted the process, and took radical action, and he was greatly rewarded.

It's easy to give up and throw in the towel. But that wasn't Nate. And it's certainly not you! Change can be really scary—especially when the desired outcome feels so far away. I am here to remind you, though, that the first step is the hardest. From there, focusing on one step at a time is the greatest way I have found to achieve goals, big or small. One step. And then another. And another. Celebrating each success—and misstep, because those are inevitable (more on that in Chapter 8)—and seeing every day as an opportunity to grow. You will get there. The road may look different than you imagined, but embrace it and enjoy the ride.

Here's the cool thing about fear: It can actually be the best push forward if you choose to see it as such. Fear keeps a lot of people stuck, and it can be difficult for them to shift perspective on this. But your mind acts like a muscle in a lot of ways, and it works out and gets stronger by practicing new ways of thinking about situations that previously stressed you out or caused you to freeze in fear. Think about it: you don't go to the gym and lift one weight and all of a sudden your body is in peak shape. The same thing goes for your thoughts.

It's only natural, then, that with the strengthening of your thoughts comes the leveling up of your actions to support them. In order for you to fully trust yourself to create a new reality and to trust that Source, God, or the Universe intends good things for you, your thoughts and actions need to work together to bring you closer to the reality you crave.

Instead of backing away from the things that scare you, practice leaning into them. I know this seems weird. But trust me when I say it truly is the only way to cultivate new ways of thinking, being, and doing in your everyday life. When something comes up that would usually make you cringe, freeze, or walk the other way, ask yourself, *What is on the other side of this feeling?*

Let's say you have a burning desire to change the world with a group of people who are positive, inspiring, and fun to be around, but you work in a cubicle by yourself, doing a job that leaves you feeling depleted and empty. You want to find something different that aligns with your heart's desires, but the thought of change and the fear of the unknown have you stuck in your current reality, not moving, wishing things were different. What if you forgot for a moment about the job that doesn't fulfill you and focused on (1) the desire for more (that fulfilling career where you're doing what you love) and (2) all the things that are on the other side of your fear of change (a purpose-driven life helping people every single day and getting paid to do so!). How does that feel? Where does that fire spark in your body? Sit with the emotions this alternate reality evokes for a moment, and instead of focusing on the *what if,* think of this as a case of *when*—because if you are committed (and I know you are, because you signed a contract!) then it's really only a matter of time before you manifest a new reality for yourself, based on your ability to exercise radical action and your refusal to settle.

Try doing that exercise in front of a mirror and watch your expression and body language change. It's powerful. And that future is possible. But to make it happen, *you* get to embrace the fear holding you back and discover a way to move toward what you truly want. As one of my favorite sayings reminds us, "If you don't like where you are, move. You are not a tree."

Decide. Commit. Take action. One small step daily is all you need to create meaningful results. Making the choice to do more of the things that put you on the path toward the life you want is worth the discomfort, don't you think? Start small if you must. The key is just to *start.*

Common Fear #3: Fear of Asking for Help

I see this all the time—people seemingly holding on to their independence by *doing it all on their own.* And I get it! It can feel difficult to reach out in a time of need and ask for help. Let's be real—it can even be difficult to admit to yourself that you need help. Why is this?

Western society in particular has developed an ideal of self-sufficiency, of capable independence. How many times have you heard stories of pioneers or immigrants who started out with virtually nothing and achieved great things, pulling themselves up by their own bootstraps? This ideal is so ingrained in our national character that it continues to be a major influence in the politics around government benefit programs and the like. If Henry Ford could do it, the reasoning goes, why can't everybody? Seems kinda silly when you think about it.

The emphasis on independence has resulted in a sense of shame when we can't do something ourselves. We've somehow equated the need for help with failure. If you need help, the myth goes, you're either stupid, weak, not resourceful, or all the above. So asking for help makes us feel vulnerable and open to all these judgments, and I've sure never met anyone who enjoyed the feeling of being judged. But the cold, hard truth is that you will be judged, whether you stay the same or make the changes necessary to live the life you want. So you might as well do what feels best for you and keep on pushing to create the legacy you feel called to create.

How about this: think about the last time someone asked *you* for help. Unless this was someone who makes a habit of imposing on you unnecessarily, I'll bet you actually felt honored to be asked. Whoever asked you for help felt safe enough with you to reveal their vulnerability, and they thought of your capabilities as the best way to accomplish the task in question.

As with so many other fears and obstacles, I have found that the most effective way of eliminating this fear is to change the way you think about asking for help. Remind yourself that the importance we put on self-reliance is a myth and tap into the feelings of empathy and community that arise in you when you yourself are asked for help. Think of reaching out as team building, not as weakness. I've discussed the ways in which living your authentic purpose will attract others of a similar vibration—well, asking for help is the most direct example of this possible.

Need more convincing? Ask anyone who's successfully battled alcoholism or another addiction. You'll find very few people who've completed such a challenging transformation without first admitting they needed help, then coming to terms with their vulnerability and *asking* for that help. So the next time you find yourself overwhelmed and in need of help, embrace it as an opportunity to stretch yourself a little bit and give the Universe the chance to show up for you.

This is what Jane did. She grew up surrounded by strong, independent women. Raised by a single mother, she spent a lot of time with her grandmother as a child while her mother was at work. Both women were vivacious, charismatic, determined, and independent in every sense of the word. Jane was told from a very young age that she could do it all on her own. She didn't need anyone's approval or acceptance, and as long as she was following her heart and leading with love, she'd be okay. This fierce independence served her for many years in many ways.

She excelled in school, got into her first-choice college, and began a company upon graduation. People often talked about her as the one who had it all together. Meanwhile, she felt trapped, alone, and scared of asking for support for fear of seeming weak. Despite the appearance that everything was okay on the outside, inside she was suffocating, and her health suffered.

For years Jane had been in relationships with great men, but in none of them had she allowed herself to be vulnerable enough to admit she simply could not do it all on her own. And more importantly, she found, she didn't *want* to do it all on her own. Not anymore. Her greatest desire was to be in a loving relationship with a man who would honor her independence while also allowing her to really express her femininity, and who would support her and take care of her when she needed it.

Jane's shift away from the fear of asking for help and appearing weak was a process. It took months of dedicated focus on creating a clear picture in her mind of what it would look like when she let go of controlling everything and allowed herself to be vulnerable, allowed herself to be taken care of, and honored others' desires to help and feel wanted and needed. It took constant practice in a variety of situations, such as letting her co-workers know she was at her limit with projects and could not take on any more; asking her partner to pick up groceries so she could take some time for herself and relax; and saying no to events in order to create boundaries and not always be on the go. It wasn't easy, but after a few months, she felt lighter, freer, and more like herself. And as she showed up more authentically and aligned in the world, the Universe mirrored back more of the same.

Today she is thriving in her relationship, openly and without shame asking for what she needs to feel safe, and has set boundaries around her personal and professional life in order to create space for more self-love and self-care. The practice of *asking* is one that she is continually partaking in, and sometimes it still feels uncomfortable. But she knows that doing this and staying committed to her *why* will bring her closer and closer to the life she is determined to live. She's reminded of this daily as opportunities unfold before her and she sees her light shining brighter than before.

Common Fear #4: Fear of Death

Finally, we come to the big one! Ever since humans developed the ability to understand our mortality, we've meditated on—and often feared—our death. When you think about it, death takes a lot of those other big fears and rolls them all up into one. If we fear appearing weak or vulnerable, we imagine that death represents the ultimate weakness, the ultimate vulnerability. If we fear change, we consider death to be the ultimate unknown. And what about light? How does fear of our own light affect the way we think about our death?

I believe that the fear of death is directly related to our fear of our own unique light. The greatest fear around death, in my experience, is that we will die before we discover our true purpose, before we're able to fully discover and express our truest, most authentic selves. Think of it—you've heard stories of people who are able to face death with complete grace and acceptance. Perhaps you've even been at the bedside of someone who exhibited this calm fearlessness. What separates such a person from someone who approaches death with fear? I'm willing to bet it has something to do with the way they *lived* more than death itself.

Does this resonate with you? Do you fear death, and do you think it might be because of your fear that the clock is ticking on your ability to connect with and share your authentic purpose with the world? This can be a difficult question to answer, because there are so many unknowns surrounding death, but the following exercise can help you figure it out.

Exercise: Plan Your Own Funeral

This is something I did years ago, and when the idea was introduced to me, I was pretty skeptical, like you may be now. But then I remembered my *why*. I came back to my purpose and the mission I was on to create the life I wanted so I could do my part to help humanity be free. And my skepticism diminished as my desire for expansion and alignment with Source grew.

We are going to go all the way in on this, so I want you to prepare yourself. Strong emotions may come up, and that's a beautiful thing. I encourage you to release any judgment you may have about this being "weird" or "not doing it right." However you experience this exercise is perfect. This is your own experience, and it's up to you whether you want to share it with someone else or allow yourself the space to *be* with yourself on this journey, right here, right now.

Go ahead and grab a piece of paper and a pen, or have your phone nearby, because you will be taking some notes. Now I invite you to close your eyes and take a deep breath. As you exhale, picture yourself in a coffin. (This will take you right past the event of death itself, the thought of the goodbyes, the anxiety of the unknown, how you got to this place, and so on.) Sit with that for a moment. Feel the coolness of your skin. Notice the calm and quiet of nothingness—or everything (it's all perspective, right?)—around you. Where do your thoughts go? Do you have any?

Slowly open your eyes. Take a long, loving, deep belly breath, and let it out with a loud, audible sigh, and think about this question: How do you want to be remembered?

Visualize the people who are at your funeral or wake. What are they saying about you? What do they remember about your life? How did you affect people? How did you show up for them? Did you love *big*? Did you love *hard*? Did you love without expectations?

Hold on to this as we continue . . . because now it's time to write your own eulogy.

Now ask yourself this: Are you happy with the vision you've created? Is this the funeral you want to have? Is this the way you want to be remembered? If not, it's not too late to change course and rewrite your story.

What can you change in your current reality in order to have the kind of funeral you truly want? For people to remember you in a way that feels good in your body, that makes you feel like you lived your purpose with intention?

My Own Funeral Vision

The above exercise became a big part of my own transformation. Not too long ago, I was involved in a leadership program where we were instructed to visualize our own funerals in detail. It was uncomfortable and, quite frankly, it was a pretty disturbing thought process to go through. What came up, though, gave me insights and clarity that I wasn't even aware I was seeking. I suddenly saw my longing to pivot and level up the way I was living my life and the way I was showing up.

I'd been working for years to come back "home" to my true self and show the world the real me. And despite all my work up to this point, the funeral I envisioned was nothing like the funeral I was hoping for somewhere in my subconscious.

In my visualization I hadn't accomplished enough and there weren't very many people there. Nothing felt authentic to the life I was growing into. It was then that I knew there was still a lot more work to do if I was truly committed to creating impact on a greater level. My vision reminded me that if I kept going at the same rate, I would be leaving behind an important piece of the big picture: that we are all *one*. Doing things on my own would never be enough, and it was because of the people around me that my life was where it was. I was overwhelmed with gratitude, and as tears streamed down my face, I recommitted to myself. I recommitted to the world.

After the process was complete, I was even more clear, and I knew that if I did something every single day to impact just one person, I could make a difference. In my past I had been so focused on material possessions and, at times, those old thoughts of needing to have the best of the best of everything in order to be loved crept in. But this reminder came at the perfect time, as they usually do, and I realized that I couldn't carry these material things with me, that what really mattered was the connection I could make with other people in an effort to impact the greater whole.

For a while I focused on living each day as if it were my last day on this planet. That may sound crazy or even a little weird, but it helped remind me to stay focused on my purpose and shut out all the noise of expectations I felt from the outside world. This new focus shifted something inside me. It lit a fire under me in a way that I needed, without even knowing it. It encouraged me to set intentions for each interaction. It forced me to really look at my decisions and question how they would create more good in the world around me.

When you start to live with the understanding that time is limited, the reality you're living in begins to change. You begin to understand that your fears are robbing you—and everyone around you—of the gift of your light. And while you don't have forever to overcome your fears, it's never too late. Even if you only manage to discover your true purpose, your authentic light, in the final hour of this life (to create an extreme example!), just think of how much better—how vastly, infinitely, endlessly superior—that story is compared to one in which you never discover it at all. The time is now. Take the power back from your fears and show the world what you're *really* made of!

Chapter 6

EMBRACE YOUR LIMITATIONS— AND THEN CRUSH THEM!

Before we begin our discussion of limitations, let me be clear about what I mean. You—the real you, at your core—are limitless. There is no end to what you can achieve or who you can be. The "limitations" we're discussing here exist in your mind, and only in your mind. As I've mentioned, they come from the way we process and internalize the expectations and roles placed upon us—wittingly or unwittingly—by anybody with influence over our lives. These beliefs can come from parents, grandparents, older siblings, teachers, coaches, clergy, and anyone else we look to for guidance on how to construct our lives, beginning literally at day one. Think back across your whole life span and try to remember all those who have offered you pieces of advice, no matter how small or seemingly insignificant at the time.

Even something as simple and sweet as *be kind to others* can be warped by an impressionable mind into a limitation if you believe it means to place others before yourself in all situations, no matter what—which, side-note, could not be further from the truth. If your intention truly is to love and be loved, to create impact and change in the world, kindness toward yourself and others will flow naturally and appropriately.

This was the case with Zach, an Ohio family man who came to Fitlife.tv seeking transformation. Zach was 110 pounds overweight, and though he was full of love and joy, he had a pattern of sabotaging his own efforts to create peace and happiness for himself. In his particular case, the problems centered around food and his family. Early on they had established a pattern of unhealthy eating—pizza, fast-food, sodas, you name it. His children, as you can imagine, looked forward to meals, because truth be told, junk food can taste delicious on our lips, even if its effect on the body, if eaten consistently over time, is deadly.

I think it's important to note before I move on that our current conditioning in this area comes from years and years of programming, reaching all the way back to our oldest ancestors. This is not to say that we do not have full control over our habits, because I believe we do, but changing them can sometimes feel pretty challenging if we have to overcome a lot of history. It's a little crazy to wrap our heads around, but the programming of our past is stored in our biology and creates subconscious patterns that can dictate our habits in the present moment. That "high" we feel, that short-term pleasure, from high-calorie, fatty, salty foods, is merely leftover programming from our hunting and gathering days. But it is still real. And because of the way it stimulates the pleasure centers of our brains, this kind of food can be addictive. So for people like Zach and his family (and many others), who were in a routine of unhealthy cravings and eating, a change in diet is a whole lot easier said than done.

Biological programming aside, where did this eating pattern stem from in Zach's own family history? After some digging he remembered how his grandparents would reward him for good behavior with food, particularly sweets! He also had memories of his parents giving him food to soothe him when he was upset, particularly when he was upset with them. So in order for him to be happy with his parents after they'd made him mad about something, he was given food instead of emotional support and love. Thus he equated food with love and acceptance, and this belief pattern solidified in his subconscious.

Without education and healthy modeling from their parents to override that programming, Zach's children craved junk food all the time. And Zach, who loved his children and wanted to make them happy, not only provided it for them but also fed himself the same thing. You can imagine how this showed up—not only with additional physical weight, but with excess emotional weight too.

In my initial conversation with Zach, he allowed himself the vulnerability to share with me the heartbreak he felt for allowing things to get so out of control. I told him it would take time and consistency on his part to upgrade his habits and show himself and his family the positive results of doing so, and as we spoke it became clear that he really felt ready to tackle this issue. I was confident I could help him.

After a few conversations, Zach became more comfortable and open in sharing how his habits had impacted his family, from his overweight children to his own embarrassment when it came to intimacy with his wife. He came to the realization that deep down he held a limiting belief that was crippling his chances at health and happiness, and ultimately he was greatly affecting his family, whom he loved dearly. Zach had been operating under the long-standing belief that in order to be liked by others, even his family, he had to give them everything they wanted. Not only did he believe he had to say yes to everyone, but he also believed he had to eat the same foods as his family or he'd face rejection or judgment.

In short, Zach was a people pleaser, as many people are. It's something I personally still struggle with at times. Maybe you can relate! And while spreading happiness and taking care of others are important parts of our life path here on earth, if you aren't taking care of yourself—if you aren't nurturing yourself in a way that lets your authentic light shine—then you are limiting the gifts you are here to share in the first place! By dimming your own unique light, you are sacrificing yourself for others, creating an exchange not based on abundance but on limited good, on one-sided benefit. People pleasing might meet your short-term needs of being liked and having surface-level harmony, but over time this kind of sacrifice can result in resentment and discord, and even mental and physical problems like the ones Zach was experiencing.

Once Zach and I discovered the limiting belief pattern that was driving him, we worked to replace it with a more positive, self-oriented declaration: *The more I treat myself with love, the more I'm loved by others.* And as we discussed in Chapter 3, loving yourself also means eating well! This realization allowed him to embrace the possibility of feeding himself the nutrients he knew his body needed without having to sacrifice the closeness he felt with his family. This change of belief shifted things so dramatically that Zach was able to lose 100 pounds over the next year. And in the process, his family became healthier, happier, and more connected. Demolishing his limiting beliefs around acceptance transformed not only his body but also his mind and spirit. And he began sharing this newfound love for himself, in his business, which doubled in revenue that same year.

Stories like Zach's are too common. Because of his childhood experiences, he held a belief that prevented him from fully living in his purpose and authenticity. But it was also a belief of Zach's—that things could be better—that allowed him to create a new reality by shifting his thoughts and practicing new ways of showing up. In other words, both the beginning and the end of his transformation story revolve around the mind's endless power! It was the power of Zach's conditioned mind that held on to his limiting beliefs, and it was also the power of his mind—once he saw the potential for his future and made the commitment to change—that was able to let those beliefs go and create a new reality not only for Zach himself but also for everyone around him.

Many of us are the same—we're our own worst enemie. But with the discovery of our limitations—with awareness instead of judgment—and a little help to turn them around, we can become our own biggest fans instead.

Letting Go of Limitations

In this chapter we'll first take a look at the mechanisms of conditioning and its connection to limiting beliefs. With an understanding of how, when, and why they arise, you'll be much better equipped to recognize limiting beliefs in yourself. Then we'll zero in on some of the most common limiting beliefs, with examples, including episodes from my own life—I've suffered from all of these at some point or another, and I'm guessing you'll be able to relate.

And then, of course, we'll look at the tools you need to start to undo the effects these limitations are having on you. If you've followed the program outlined in this book so far, you've already developed one of the most powerful tools available: commitment. You've committed to new practices, to your body, mind, and spirit, and to the journey that will carry you from where you are to where you want to be. In the examples below, I'll provide you with some more exercises you can use.

A mentor can be another powerful tool. Just as Frank helped me identify my own limitations and discover my purpose, there might be someone you could reach out to who could help you do the same on your own personal journey. If that is your wish, send that call out into the Universe, and then be watchful for signs that someone is drawing near to assist you.

There are also many personal development courses available—intensive, in-person versions of the program I've outlined here. Do a little research in your area and consider whether one of these might be right for you. There are also some great personal development courses available online these days. Find what resonates with you, and invite a buddy to join you!

With clarity and the right combination of approaches, you'll develop the skills to crush these limitations and to keep on crushing them when they make their inevitable attempts at a comeback. It's my firm belief that if you commit fully to this process, you'll be able not only to stop the harm those limitations have been causing but also to convert them into fuel (or motivation) for positive change.

Getting Ready for the Cold, Hard Truth

Before we get to the hard work of this chapter, I'd like to take a few moments for preparation. The process of identifying your limitations and their sources calls for radical honesty. You might have to face difficult truths about your parents, teachers, and perhaps even your spouse or other people you love. You will likely have to face difficult truths about yourself too. It's time to get brutally honest about how you are showing up in the world and your actual ways of being. And while this might be painful, I know you'll be able to get through it—and preserve your relationships with your loved ones and yourself in the process as you come from a place of acceptance and compassion. So leave your judgments behind—they won't serve you here. And know that wherever you picked up your limitations, you picked them up for a reason. Even if you were mistreated or abused, like I was, remember that it all had a purpose and look back on it with love and gratitude for the person you are now and the growth opportunities that remain in your path because of it. With this perspective you'll be able not only to identify your limitations and the problems they're causing but also to visualize the potential of your life beyond them.

The first step is figuring out just who you are and where you stand right now, today. This means identifying and facing your thought patterns—limiting and otherwise—and that requires a bit of time travel. So get ready to head right into your inner child—your earliest, most formative memories, your innermost core.

Childhood Conditioning

We are born into this world with subconscious patterns formed by conditioning in utero. The thoughts of our parents, particularly any stressors they may feel during pregnancy, leave impressions on our growing human form as we are transformed from a small seed into a body, preparing to come into an unknown world. Kind of wild to think about, isn't it? We take on energy in the womb just as we take on (and emit) energy once we are free to roam the landscape of earth in our human form. Even as a little seed, we have the power to take on limiting beliefs, scarcity, and anything going on in the reality around us. This includes fears or beliefs of lack. All can be transmitted into our being as we are forming limbs, organs, our human form, all while inside our mother's womb.

Subconsciously you felt it in your cells as you were growing, and maybe you still feel it. In the end it becomes part of you, and so often you are taking it as your own belief system, when in fact it may not be yours at all. You were conditioned from before you were even aware of your own thoughts. Talk about the power of the mind!

The conditioning doesn't stop there. As children we are supremely adaptable. We have to be—the world is run by adults, and without their size, strength, abilities, resources, or freedom, our best tool for survival is to ensure that we live our lives in ways that make people want to take care of us. This means adapting and sometimes even contorting ourselves to the expectations and needs of others. This goes on for years. In fact, childhood in humans lasts longer than the entire average life span of many other species. This means we get years—*decades*, in some cases—of practice living our lives as others teach us to. And over the years those lessons become so much a part of us that we no longer notice they're there.

Of course, many of these lessons are helpful. Without parents or teachers or other role models, we'd be at a complete loss as to how to function. But those lessons, as well-intended as they might have been, are not always in alignment with who we really are. When they aren't aligned and we adapt to them anyway, the shadow gets a little bigger and blocks a little more of our light, creating an imbalance that we begin to feel more and more over time.

Rather than shedding these limitations when we get to adulthood, we carry them with us. And when we are confronted with the big choices of adulthood, like which career to pursue, what our relationships should provide for us, and how to raise our own children, those limitations are still there, influencing our every decision and guiding us toward the things we were taught to pursue rather than toward our true desires.

Fast-forward to your life now. Maybe you have abusive relationships and you wonder why. Or you carry fears of things you have never experienced personally and it makes no sense to you why this is such an issue. Here's the truth: The impression becomes the expression. All those things you absorbed, from the moment of your conception (or even in your past lives, if you believe in that) up to this present moment, become the same things you both emit and attract. With this awareness, though, comes the freedom to choose better, to elevate and align your experience to that which leaves you feeling empowered and joyful.

My Own Conditioning

The lack of love I was shown by my biological parents and a general sense of scarcity conditioned me to believe my self-worth depended on exterior circumstances. I felt like everyone was going to abandon me—not just my dad but also my mom and anyone I thought was supposed to love me. It affected my relationships for a very long time. And there are moments in my adult life when this still creeps in, despite the work I have done and continue to do.

The value of financial success was also a big conditioned belief for me, because somewhere inside I believed if I had more of it, I could control everything within and around me. Somehow I even believed that financial abundance would heal my heart and fix the lingering pain. And so I chased money. Because this goal was not in alignment with my purpose, I was in a state of constant discord, and my physical and mental health both suffered as a consequence.

Instead of judging these limitations, though, I now give thanks for them, because it was from this place that I was able to come back to myself and separate what is mine from what I was conditioned to believe based on others' fears and truths. This has been very powerful for me to sit with and absorb, and I know it can be for you too.

Beyond Conditioning

If you have issues or limiting beliefs that keep recurring, it's time to get honest and examine how you were conditioned as a child and take steps toward letting those things go. You are not a prisoner to your conditioning. Changing how you react to your reality and how you choose to live in the present moment is up to you.

As I explained previously, Zach's early conditioning taught him that his worth depended on his ability to create happiness and harmony for those around him, even if it meant neglecting himself. Because of these beliefs, his physical and mental health suffered, just as mine did. The means of achieving the illusion of success or happiness or whatever you're chasing may look different, but when the truth of the matter doesn't align with who you are at your deepest level, the outcome is always the same: disconnection, dissatisfaction, a feeling of emptiness, and, at some level, poor health.

To break this pattern, you must identify your limitations from a place of awareness and acceptance. This often means naming the limitations' sources with love and releasing them one by one until you feel free and like yourself, maybe even for the first time. By identifying what these limitations are and where they come from, you can then create a plan to raise your vibration and bring in healthier thoughts and actions to cultivate the life experience you desire. When you commit to the shift and you begin moving one step at a time toward more of what you want from a place of knowing versus what you have always done, magic unfolds. And this time it feels good. It feels right. It feels like home.

Let's take a look at some of the biggest limitations I've seen with my clients and our community as a whole. Chances are you will relate to at least one of these. And if not one of these specifically, I'm certain you will identify with the feelings or emotions that arise from having limitations that have been holding you back and keeping you from living out your full potential.

Common Limitation #1: Lack of Self-Worth

Self-worth is the sense that you matter—that your ideas and actions are valuable to others, and not just to those in your immediate circle, but as a component of your whole community, even as an indispensable piece of the Universe. Without belief in your own self-worth, you won't stand up for yourself. You won't strive for the things you want, because you'll believe you don't deserve them.

Why are so many of us afflicted with low self-worth? This limitation is pervasive because we are constantly immersed in systems that compare us to others and cause us to question our value, beginning at a very young age. It often begins with our parents, like so many things do. If you were ever told that you or your efforts weren't good enough, your self-worth suffered a blow. Even if your parents were warm and completely accepting, when you went off to school, if you weren't the top student in every class, you learned that other people's deeds had more value than yours did. After school this system of comparison does not diminish but only changes shape slightly, replacing grades with status, salary, and fame as the methods of scorekeeping.

To make things worse, we as a culture are obsessed with the rich and the famous, the high-status individuals to whom entire publications and television shows are devoted: this family or that family, the housewives of this city or that city. If you are an average person with an average salary and an average career, how are you supposed to feel about your self-worth in a celebrity-crazed culture? For argument's sake let's say you're even somebody who does extraordinary work. Perhaps you're a nurse in an emergency department who contributes to life-saving efforts daily. Or maybe you're a teacher or counselor who puts in hours every week to transform the lives of at-risk children. Well, according to the always-pervasive news feeds, your efforts are worth a whole lot less than the bathing suit choice of the latest Instagram phenomenon.

My own childhood conditioning caused me some serious struggles in this department. The abuse I suffered led me to believe I wasn't worthy of love, and beyond that I saw my biological parents fighting frequently, often teetering on the brink of divorce. As a result of this modeling, I went on to attract relationships for myself that could be quite difficult. Sometimes I wanted to pull my hair out. But it's all been a result of my own conditioning, my own feelings of self-worth.

If you can relate to this, what do you do to radically boost your self-worth, to understand that you are every bit as worthy as anyone else? It all starts with your self-talk. Think about the narrative that runs through your head on a daily basis. What do you tell yourself about your decisions, your behaviors, your abilities? What do you focus on?

We humans have a tendency to focus on the negative. If you're having trouble paying a bill on time, for example, you might well spend a day or two beating yourself up about it, doubting your abilities and the wisdom of your decisions. But what about all the bills you *did* manage to pay on time, all the other months you got all your bills paid, all the hard work you put in to earn the money to do just that? And what about all the other things you accomplished? You got the kids to school on time with their lunches packed, addressed the CHECK ENGINE light on your dashboard, took a friend out to dinner for her birthday even though you'd had a long day already, and on and on . . .

You are an amazing individual whose days are full of valuable deeds, and you get to allow those deeds to define your self-worth as well. So remember to celebrate yourself often and without reservations! Give yourself a pat on the back every time you achieve a small victory, even if someone else might say you're "just doing your job." Because you know what? Your "job" is worth celebrating! Yes, it's your responsibility to get your kids up and dressed and get their lunches packed and get them out the door, through the traffic or the snow (uphill both ways!) to school—but that's an awesome responsibility. Your kids are learning a great deal from how you show up, and the lessons they're learning will affect those they interact with, who will in turn affect others. And the cycle continues on and on with each action or inaction you choose.

Get the picture? If you're like most people, you're overlooking a hundred things every day that you could draw strength and self-worth from. Figure out what these are and make it a point to acknowledge them. Make a game out of it, even! For instance, decide, *When I accomplish* _____ , *I will reward myself with* _____ . And stick to your promise to yourself!

Exercise: Rewrite the Inner Critic's Script

This exercise will provide you with a better understanding of how you view your own self-worth so that you can identify whether or not this limitation applies to you. What are the voices you hear when you're by yourself? Set a timer for five minutes and write out all the voices you hear in your head during that time. Don't worry about spelling, grammar, punctuation, or any of that—the goal is to write as quickly as you can to catch the flow and pattern of your thoughts. If judgment comes up, acknowledge it and move through it—don't allow yourself to get stuck in these simple-minded thoughts. After five minutes go back over what you've written. Pay close attention to the vibration of your language. Is it confident or full of doubt? Is it critical? Do you disparage yourself? Do you find negativity? Are you using words like *can't, won't, shouldn't?*

Now rewrite that flow of consciousness, transforming any doubt or negativity into confidence and positivity. Write your thoughts as if your abilities are supreme and your plans or goals are critical and inevitable pieces of the Universe—which they are!

Here's an example of what I mean:

Negative self-talk: *I don't have enough money to live the life I want. I never have enough time to do the things I want. I am overweight because I don't have energy to go to the gym. I eat bad food because it's cheaper than healthy food and it's easier . . .*

You could reframe this as: *I am grateful for the life I am living. I have more than enough time for the things that are important to me. I still have some work to do to achieve the body I feel most comfortable in and I am grateful to love myself enough to make time for healthy habits, like moving my body and fueling myself with whole foods. I create my reality and I am committed to my growth.*

As you move back out of the exercise and into your regular daily activities, try to continue catching your doubt and negativity and alter it. If you keep at it, you can literally change the way you think with this new awareness.

Common Limitation #2: Fear

A definition of fear seems hardly necessary—we're all acquainted with the feeling from a very young age! Fear is an evolutionary holdover from a time in human history when serious danger was everywhere. Predators, tribal warfare, disease, and environmental hazards were all a part of daily life. We evolved a fear response to boost our awareness and put our muscles in a state of readiness to either defend ourselves or to run away—the famous "fight-or-flight" response. A million years ago, the adrenaline dump of a fear response was a necessary part of survival.

For many of us in modern society, very few of these life-threatening hazards remain. However, our bodies still respond with the same reaction, frequently putting us in states of anxiety over the much smaller threats of modern life. Of course, catastrophic circumstances can still arise. Car wrecks and violent crime are daily occurrences, unfortunately, and thousands upon thousands are locked in various armed conflicts around the globe. But for the rest of us, we're responding to things like career uncertainties and relationship drama with the same level of fear once reserved for the approach of a hungry grizzly bear.

So instead of helping us with survival, our fear ends up being used for other things, like protecting our egos and confining us to the perceived safety of our habits and routines—which in turn keep us from stretching out and discovering the full extent of our true selves.

The way to overcome fear is actually quite similar to the way to overcome anything. Recognize that it exists in the first place, acknowledge it, and accept the truth that it may be holding you back, that your fear is simply a protective state, not something serving you in the way you believe it is. Now reframe it, just as you did in the self-worth exercise. This is what I do every time I notice fear creeping in and trying to hold me back. For example:

Fear: *Everyone always leaves me, so to stay safe I will keep my walls up and only allow people in so far. That way I won't get hurt.*

Other side of fear: *I attract people and experiences that fuel my heart and purpose. I feel safe to share my light authentically, and because of this I attract more of the same, creating abundant, impactful, loving relationships.*

Common Limitation #3: "I Can't"

"It's just not possible for me." Sound familiar? How many times have you said no to life simply because you didn't believe it was possible for you to accomplish the task at hand? Instead of making an attempt and risking failure, you just . . . *didn't.*

I remember an instance when I was asked to write a story as a kid. I had never done this before, and although now writing is like second nature to me, it seemed impossible at the time! "I can't" was my initial reaction. My teacher sat next to me and explained that I was capable of anything. I just had to practice and over time I would get better. She was right.

But that self-doubt monster, he's a real pest at times. And sometimes you gotta look him straight in the eye and kindly excuse yourself with a smile. As I have mentioned numerous times, you are capable of anything you put your mind to. Those self-imposed limitations are completely false, and they're designed to keep you stuck instead of expanding.

What are the areas in your life where you feel you just *can't do* or *can't be* or *can't have* or *can't_____*? Read this next part slowly: You *can* because you *are*. You are the light; you are a part of the universal whole; and you were designed with endless powers, some of which you've tapped into and some of which still remain for you to discover and explore. So hold to your commitment to do just that. Your desire for a more loving existence for the betterment of yourself and all those around you and all humanity—these are all possible. And if you desire it, you can make it a reality. It's not about *if*—it's about *when*.

You can. Because you are.

Exercise: Hold the Vision

This exercise will help you identify your limitations and teach you the practice of visualizing your life beyond them. This is not a one-time exercise—rather, the more you can do this, the faster those limitations will fall away. I would recommend starting and ending each day with this exercise, in fact.

The first step is to create a vision of your life just as you want it to be. Hold that vision in your mind, whether it consists of goals for your career, health, relationships, or whatever else you're committed to transforming. Once it's firmly fixed in your mind, think about what would be required for you to realize that vision. Do you hear those objections arising in your mind? Write them down. Those are your false limitations!

We're not going to stop there, though—in order to truly crush your limitations, you've got to make sure you identify all of them. Choose three people who know you better than anybody and ask them where they see you holding yourself back. Do you have any blind spots? Add these things to your list.

Now we're going to work on transforming those limitations. Take your list, and for each item, write down the following:

- A counterstatement.

- A message of gratitude.

- One action you can take immediately to start shifting your limitation.

For example, let's say your true desire is to travel the world, but you believe you'll never have enough money to do it. On your list of limitations, you'd write, *I don't have enough money*. And beneath that:

- *My life is full of abundance.*

- *Thank you, Universe, for providing me a space to create whatever I want in this life. Thank you for all the things I do have: a roof over my head, food in my belly, meaningful relationships.*

- *I can eat out less to save money.*

In this way you'll begin to remove these limitations, these anchors to the former version of yourself, and you'll begin to take real action toward your true desires. Each time you focus on the counterstatement instead of the limitation, each time you meditate on that sense of gratitude, and each time you follow through on one of those actions, your light shines a little brighter.

PART III

Own Your Awesome

You've come so far, and here you are, facing the light at the end of the tunnel. Look at that! I knew you could do it. You're so close to the freedom you crave, so stay the course. I promise there are great things in store for you. In fact, I am willing to bet you are already seeing some of your hard work paying off!

If you've been doing the work I've suggested in Parts I and II, then you're feeling a shift within and realizing that there really is hope. There may still be a ways to go to get to your goals, and that's okay. You've discovered what has been holding you back and have outlined some action steps to catapult you into the next phase beautifully. The aim is not to have it all figured out. The aim is to have a better understanding of how you got here in the first place and a plan to crawl out of hiding and finally step into the you that has been hiding. The you that was perfectly placed here, right now, with purpose.

Part III is about owning your awesome—tapping into the light inside you and allowing it to shine out, far and wide, into every aspect of your life. We'll take your new-found awareness of your strengths and continue building on them. At this point in the journey, there is still a temptation to backslide into your old habits and ways of being, so it's critical to actively push yourself forward and stay engaged with the process of transformation. This is the time to get creative with developing new positive habits and to really embrace all the wonderful opportunities that await your true self.

In Chapter 7 you'll learn to create your soul map—your vision for your whydentity. You'll learn about vision casting, clarity, and belief, which are the tools you'll use to keep yourself moving forward. Chapter 8 will cover ways to keep building momentum so new habits don't seem like an effort anymore—so that this transformation becomes your new way of being and your course becomes unshakable. Chapter 9 is about tapping into Source, which means fully embracing your light and unconditionally loving, accepting, and forgiving your true self, both the light and the dark. Finally, we'll end with a look at our togetherness, and the powerful knowledge that a commitment to love yourself is the same as a commitment to love others.

That's right—it's time to let in the first real waves of that hope and joy that have seemed so elusive. With some mindfulness, some positivity, and your continued commitment, you will be able to convert your efforts into some all-important momentum. That momentum in turn will help you build new, positive, sustainable habits and transform this mind-set you have worked so hard to establish into a natural, effortless state of being. Yes, you're almost there—but we are not going to slow down now! Together we will continue working on recognizing and celebrating your light until nobody and nothing can dim it ever again.

Exercise: Progress Check

Before we go on, let's take a moment after all the hard work in Part II to step back and reconnect with the big picture. Below is a set of questions. As you read through them, don't worry too much about coming up with specific answers. Rather, do a quick check of whatever feelings each question triggers. Do you have an immediate answer? What's your confidence level in your answer? What are the things you still have to learn about yourself? Pay special attention to the questions where you feel a little stumped—that's where the biggest potential progress lies. Set an intention to search for those answers, and let that intention guide you through the rest of the journey. Now make yourself comfortable, take a few deep breaths, get rid of all judgments (because that's how we do in *You Be You*), and ask yourself:

- Am I in alignment with my soul?
- What in my life is draining my energy? What is adding energy?
- When am I in my highest vibration? During the day or at night?
- Am I asking for guidance from Source daily?
- Am I eating in a way that fuels my highest self?
- Am I continually striving to elevate my mind and way of thinking?
- Am I removing toxic relationships?
- Am I committed to fulfilling a legacy? What does that commitment look like?
- What would it look like to receive? How would this feel?
- What would it look like if I lived out my commitment (remember that contract) every day? What kinds of opportunities would be possible?

- How do I want to feel?
- How can I stay with my bigger vision?
- How can I stay consistent?
- How can I connect to God, Source, the Universe, to get the answers I seek?
- What daily, soul-expanding ritual needs to be in place in order for my wings to open and allow me to fly?
- Who do I need to become to fulfill my destiny, my soul's desire and purpose?

Chapter 7

SOUL MAPPING

All right, we're going to get a little woo-woo in this chapter. You have been working hard so far, digging around in your past, confronting all your (false!) limitations, re-evaluating your relationships, and facing down your demons with conviction and determination. That's all hugely important, but I think you'd agree with me that it isn't necessarily a whole lot of fun.

It's time to change all that. We're going to do nothing short of using the power of your mind to blow your future right open. I'm talking about redefining time itself and becoming the master of the infinity of dimensions in which we all exist. This is the much-anticipated self-empowerment phase.

Remember back in Chapter 2 when you worked on discovering your whydentity? That, of course, is your true purpose, upon which the new and improved version of yourself lies. That was a powerful discovery, but I'm not letting you stop there. Your whydentity is just the surface of what I like to call your soul map. I'll get back to that in a minute, but first we need to change the way you think about time.

So what is time? In one sense it's a linear system we use to organize our experiences. Some things happen, and after that other things happen, and then after that maybe we have an appointment for a fancy lunch (fun!) or the DMV (not so much!). It gets dark, we go to sleep, it gets light, and we wake up and run through the routine again.

But in another sense, that's all just an illusion. It's a system we made up because it matches our sensory perceptions, and it's so much easier to just deal with what seems to be in front of us rather than digging deeper.

In the soul space, time is much different. It isn't constrained by linear notions. Instead, everything possible— and I mean *everything*—is happening all at once, in this and in all other dimensions. If this is your first introduction to such an idea, don't worry too much about wrapping your head around this mind-blowing theory. Here's the takeaway: That future you envision, where you're living an all-encompassing, richly fulfilling life based on your deepest purpose? *It's already happening somewhere in your reality.* You're already living it, even if you don't see and feel it right now. It isn't just some future possibility, it's a real path, accessible immediately. I don't mean to say that you've simply been coming home from work and going to the wrong house, of course. But what I am getting at is that there is a reality to your visions that goes well beyond insubstantial hopes and plans for your seemingly hard-to-reach future.

This is where a soul map comes in. A soul map is what you get when you take your whydentity—your truest purpose—and couple it with the concept of time as merely illusory. When you marry these two powerful truths, you realize that your purpose is something that truly transcends your life. It existed before you were born, and it will continue to exist even after the physical vessel you've been given to inhabit during this cycle releases your spirit. Your ideal life also exists in this space. There really is no end and no beginning. It just *is*. That ideal life is right there, always, just to one side or the other, and all you have to do is shift your thinking to access it.

All right, Drew, you're thinking. *I suppose now you're going to give me the magical tools I need to make this radical shift?*

One—there's nothing magical about them. (Well, maybe a little.) Two—of course I am! You didn't think I was just going to toss that out there and bail, did you? This chapter will provide you with a set of incredibly powerful techniques to help you not only envision your purpose-driven life but also close the gap between where you are and where you want to be.

Vision Casting

Vision casting is a powerful technique that rests on the belief that whatever dream, desire, or goal we have in our hearts is possible, and when we resonate that frequency, we cause it to be fulfilled. This process expands us beyond our present moment and allows us to join with the highest version of ourselves. It works by creating visions, which then create feeling responses in the body and shifts in the subconscious, which in turn begin to attract the reality of those visions. How does this relate to our previous discussion of time as an illusion? The power of this technique comes from the knowledge that your transformation is already complete. Your vision has already come to pass. Everything has already come together in perfect harmony and alignment. Let's get down to some specifics on this, so you can get going with casting your own vision and actualizing all that you desire!

So what's the distinction between simply visualizing or daydreaming and vision casting? There are two major differences: intention and clarity.

The intention behind a mere visualization or daydream can vary. It might be a simple diversion, something entertaining for your mind when you're stuck in a long, boring meeting, for example. It might be recreational, like when you buy a lottery ticket—though you don't really expect to win, you might still enjoy dreaming of giant yachts or huge mansions. On a more practical level, you might use visualization to help you make a decision, such as which shirt to buy. You visualize yourself in each of the shirts, imagine which one makes you feel better, and then make your choice.

The intention behind vision casting, however, is much different: it is nothing short of creating an entire reality. This entails shifts in your thoughts, both conscious and subconscious, and in your emotional state, and above all it requires a commitment to action—a commitment that you'll take the steps you've been putting off or avoiding altogether.

One of my earliest experiences with this came just after high school, when I was 17. At the time I wasn't abundant in all areas of my life, but I knew it was possible because I saw others doing it. I saw people with the lifestyle I wanted, which kept me hungry for more and kept my soul sizzling with hope. I set an intention to change my circumstances, and I took what action I could.

I set up my schedule like I thought an adult would: an early morning wake-up, a typical nine-to-five workday, and set times for lunch and short breaks. This structure, I figured, would help me get used to the "real world," at least by corporate standards. I really believe preparing myself in this way played a part in me ultimately landing my first "official" job: putting commercial roofing on grocery stores and earning $20 an hour, which was a lot for 1990s Michigan. Later I found out it wasn't actually legal to employ a 17-year-old for that sort of work, but that didn't take away the pride I felt to be making my own way and creating financial means for myself or the newfound sense of freedom and independence it brought me. My intention had been clear: to make money so I could do the things I wanted to do. And because of this intention and the actions I took to make it a reality, it happened.

The second piece of the puzzle is clarity. Your reality, after all, is built from specifics and details, not from vague general ideas. When you are daydreaming about your lottery winnings, it's fine to be unclear about whether your dream home will have a pool and a hot tub, or a walk-in closet and a beautiful garden, or all of the above. When you are vision casting, though, you get to create all of it straight from your mind: the sights, the sounds, the tastes, the smells, the textures, the emotions, and everything else that comes with realizing your dream. If you are vague about the details, the Universe will have a hard time responding. Bottom line: if you're confused, the Universe will be too.

Think of it this way: Your job here is very much like that of a novelist's or movie director's. You get to create a world so realistic and detailed that it will transport the audience entirely and create a whole new existence for them. In this case, though, you are also the star and the primary audience member. (The rest of the audience consists of everyone in your life who will be swept up into your new existence—friends, family, future co-workers, and so on.) So think about the last good book you read or the last good movie you saw. Was the setting specific or vague? Did you have a clear image of the characters, or were they featureless mannequins? Obviously, vague doesn't work. It knocks the audience right out of the story and back into their current reality. It's a reminder that everything they are seeing is an illusion, which takes the fun out of it!

The same principles apply to you when you're vision casting. If you're unclear about what you want, some part of you will have a hard time fully seeing it as a possibility. Your commitment to the vision will vanish, and you'll pop right up out of your chair to head to the snack bar instead. If, on the other hand, you use the more-than-capable powers of your incredible mind to create a new, all-encompassing reality, you will be so convinced of it that it will shift and spark inspiration in every part of your body, all the way down to your very cells!

This is where true transformation becomes possible. Once you begin to actually *see* and *feel* your dreams on the deepest level of your spirit and with your entire being, the awareness around your unlimited potential on this planet will affect all your decisions. There will be no other choice but to realize your vision; it will encompass your every thought and action simply because you will know it's exactly *why* you are here (you know, the whole whydentity thing). It will change how you see yourself and therefore how others see you. Creating this clarity will take some serious practice trusting yourself and the Universe to fully support your desires. It will also take you staying open and practicing nonattachment to the *how*. Remember, there are many different routes to reach any destination. Keep focusing on your *why*. And keep opening yourself to the signs as they arise, because they will show up.

Vision casting is your time to immerse yourself fully in the vision of who you want to be and what you want to achieve, seeing yourself as if you have already achieved it. Let's say, for example, that you are working on vision casting to transform your career path. Think about the position you would like to have and take yourself through an entire day in your mind, and don't skimp on the details. See yourself waking up. Where do you live? Who are you sleeping next to? How luxurious do those sheets with an obscenely high thread count feel? Now rise and shine and take yourself through your morning routine. What time is it? How do you feel? What do you do? What do you eat? What do you wear? What thoughts are in your head? Now leave the house. How do you get to work? How do you feel when you walk through the door? Who is there, and how do they greet you? Or maybe you're the boss, and you are the first one to walk through the door. How does it feel?

I think you get the picture (literally!). And that's just one morning of one typical day. Think also about how you'll spend holidays, where you'll go on vacation, and what you'll have for dinner on your last night in whatever island or mountain lodge or Parisian restaurant you cast yourself into. Think of the conversations you'll have, the people you'll meet, the world of opportunities that will be continuously open for you in your new reality. And do it with the intention to make it all real, the commitment to steady action, and with the absolute conviction that it will all come to pass just as you imagine it.

It is equally important to be absolutely clear on the things that you do *not* want. Life is rarely straightforward, and course corrections are necessary throughout, so it will greatly aid your transformation if you can achieve full clarity on what you're choosing to avoid. When I lived in Tampa, for example, and I was just beginning my journey, there was a great deal I loved about the city. The gulf setting is beautiful, the city contained the people who had really embraced me and my business, and it was there where I met perhaps my greatest mentor, Frank. But at the same time, I knew there was a lot about Tampa that wasn't in alignment with my growing sense of purpose and mission. It was where I had developed friendships that helped me hide from my own light and that contributed to a lifestyle that came far short of my greatest potential. Recognizing these things led me not only to leave the city, but to move all the way across the country to a new place, where I could inhabit a new physical space, just as I discussed in the opening of this chapter.

As your belief in yourself grows and you begin to really live in your purpose daily, you will more clearly recognize your self-imposed limitations and it will become easier and easier to crush them! You will find yourself making decisions with confidence when it comes to events and relationships that are in alignment with your vision and those that aren't. It is critical to act on them both. You might have to sever relationships that once seemed integral to your being. You might decide to turn your back on a successful career, just as Djamel did. You might even choose to move clear across the country, like I did. Only by trusting your vision and your gut will you create a future more magnificent than you ever thought possible. And though some of the resulting decisions may feel difficult, or even painful, your commitment and conviction to carry out your vision, and the clarity of your purpose, will help you not only get through them but come out on the other side stronger than ever.

So how exactly does vision casting transform your desires into a present-moment reality? The same way a novel or a movie is created—by putting yourself where you want to be, one moment at a time. Back to the teenage version of me, for a moment: I remember asking myself, *What do all the successful people have in common?* As I thought about it and began paying closer attention, I realized that in all the movies, television shows, and advertisements, wealthy people always had classical music playing. Well, I had an Isuzu at the time, so I'd roll around my hometown of Lake City, listening to Beethoven, pretending I was driving a Rolls-Royce. Looking back, I have to laugh. As I have mentioned before, there was a time in my life when I was chasing money. But the thing is, even this simple—and kind of humorous—routine that I cultivated heightened my state of flow and intention, allowing me to imagine more for my life. Just that change of music helped me level up my mind-set when it came to subconsciously creating a bigger vision and ultimately a bigger reality for my life. Try this for yourself! Research shows that music can be effective at regulating both arousal and mood as well as boosting self-awareness, both of which will go far in supporting you on your transformation journey.

Another great exercise to further support your growth is to shift by leveling up your surroundings. My favorite example of this was a suggestion from another mentor of mine, who pointed out that where I chose to buy my coffee each morning could shift my perspective on a much greater scale. I had no idea what he meant at first, but as he pointed out, a coffee at Starbucks costs about the same as a coffee at the Ritz-Carlton. He suggested I go to the places that embodied how I wanted to feel and experience this firsthand. And he was right! I began searching for ways to buy my coffee while surrounded by wealth (which was what I desired more at the time because it's what I felt I was lacking) and that brought me to the very place he mentioned for the full Ritz experience! It felt different—I felt different.

The lessons of this story hold true for all areas of your life. Go to the places that embody your dreams and experience the feelings as you soak in your surroundings and the type of people you want to be around. Think about the choices you make daily and whether or not they're supporting your journey of transformation.

I am not saying you have to drink your coffee at the Ritz to get where you want to go. What I *am* saying is that every single decision you make will either move you closer to or farther away from the life you desire. So ask yourself: Are you someone who has coffee at the dime-a-dozen franchise on the corner, or at the Ritz? Neither is right or wrong. It's about what feels authentic and true to the person you are at your core—the *you* that you are stepping into. The choice is yours.

And the outcome of your journey is based on the choices you make every moment of every day.

Wow Goggles

Here's another tool you can use to help heighten the sense of life's endless potential all around you. Every morning when you wake up, put on your *wow goggles*—a term I like to use for our inherent sense of amazement and wonder. With our fast-paced lifestyles, removing these often becomes a subconscious act, but if you can remind yourself to put them back on, the world comes alive again in incredible ways.

This dirty juice glass before me? Without wow goggles it's just a chore I have to do. But with my goggles on? Some mind-blowingly brilliant genius figured out how to *make this thing out of sand!* That annoying drive to work? *A series of millions of harnessed explosions that propel you across the most elaborate transportation network in human history.*

Remind yourself as much as possible to view the world as if it's the first time and the last time you will ever see it—and then even the simplest of chores, like brushing your teeth, becomes an absolute miracle. So put on those wow goggles and look around. Find the joy and gratitude in each experience that comes your way.

Segment Intending

The next tool I want to share with you is a version of vision casting, designed to transform a single chunk—or segment—of your day. It's essentially the same process, though: you create a clear intention for the future, and then you commit to transforming that vision into reality. It's called *segment intending*, and it comes to us from the Abraham-Hicks teachings. It's one of my personal favorite techniques to create abundance in every moment of my day, and I think you'll find it hugely beneficial too.

A "segment" is a portion of your day when you have a given intention, like making breakfast or getting the kids to school or commuting to work. Segment intending is the practice of being deliberate about defining the vibration of each of those segments beforehand—which causes a shift in your entire way of being that induces the Universe to shift as well to help you create the segment you want. In essence, it's putting yourself in charge of your every moment, rather than letting your moments knock you around.

You probably already do a version of this for certain things in your life. Let's say, for example, that you're planning for an important meeting. You rehearse the things you need to say, and you think about the way others will react to you and the meeting's possible outcomes. If you're like most people, you will also have some anxiety mixed in with this, as you think about saying the wrong thing or failing to get your point across or not producing the intended results. How would your thought process change if you knew you had the power to create the outcome you want just with clarity of thought and intention? You would immediately drop the anxiety and you would put all that energy into scripting out the best possible scenario. That's segment intending. This technique strips away any power that the unknown, or fear, has over you, and transforms it into a force for positive creation.

But we are not done yet! Segment intending can transform literally any portion of your day. Even the parts that seem mundane now or are often overlooked. Let's take that too-common example of a nasty commute. Twice-daily doses of tangled traffic and honking horns present enough frustrations on their own, but it gets even worse—the dread of that commute alone can infect the other parts of your day, spreading anxiety and discomfort into what might otherwise be a calm breakfast or a productive afternoon at your desk.

But what if segment intending could transform all this? Think of all the possibilities those commute segments of your day might present. You could change the vibration of that time in your car to one of education and growth, in which case you might take advantage of the widespread availability of podcasts and other audio content to become an expert in nearly any subject imaginable. You could listen to novels, study the complete works of Chopin, even learn a new language in that time. Or you might set an intention to create a problem-solving vibration, and you could use that time to set your brain to work on finding creative solutions to problems at work, at home, or elsewhere in your life. You might use that time for meditation and simply focus on taking deep breaths and centering yourself—a commute where you consciously draw in a few hundred deep breaths is going to deliver you to your destination with a much calmer mind than a commute where you allow yourself to be annoyed and stressed out about traffic, which, let me remind you, you have absolutely no control over. Your breath and reaction to your circumstances, though, are all yours. The key here is to intentionally take charge of your time, rather than letting your time dictate your emotional state.

And then when you arrive at work or wherever your destination may be, another segment begins. How do you spend that first half hour? Maybe you routinely show up 10 minutes late, then spend another 10 minutes getting coffee and chatting idly, and then another 10 minutes shuffling things around on your desk. But is that how you would script things each day if you created a conscious intention to make that first half hour as great as it could possibly be? Of course not. With clear intentions and commitment and only a few minutes of forethought, I bet you could quadruple your productivity, giving yourself more time at the end of the day for some self-care or simply doing more of the things you enjoy.

So now, all of a sudden, and with very little effort, you've supercharged your commute and the beginning of your work day. What do you think would happen if you were to string more and more of these intentional segments together? You'd become more effective at work, so your career and opportunities would improve. You'd become more present with other people, so your relationships would improve. You'd become more an inhabitant of the present moment, so your anxiety and stress levels would decrease. You'd become more deliberate about how you feed and exercise your body, so your health would improve. And each one of these aspects levels up all the others, so if you were to stay with it, you'd create an upward spiral of positive transformation. In other words your light would get brighter and brighter.

I get excited just *thinking* about these techniques and all they can bring you! What is possible for you and every human being on this planet is endless, truly. There is *no* limit to living the life you desire as the real you. One day at a time. One foot in front of the other, with clarity and intention.

The Power of Gratitude

So now you have used vision casting to create your soul map and you are using vision casting and segment intending to create your future, and the Universe is responding to the clarity of your vision, your undeniable intentions, and your productive actions. There's only one more ingredient required to complete this loop and create a constant cycle of resonating positivity, and that's gratitude. With mindful thankfulness you acknowledge the Universe's gift of abundance, which in turn supports the clarity of your vision and the level of your commitment, which creates more abundance, which creates more opportunities for gratitude, and so on.

Some people practice gratitude through some type of meditation, setting aside a part of each day to meditate on all the things they are blessed to be grateful for. I like to do this before I even get out of bed. As soon as I wake up, my mind goes straight to all the opportunities of the upcoming day and the lives I'll be fortunate enough to touch. By the time my feet hit the floor, I am so filled with gratitude at the prospects of the coming day and for my own journey that I'm able to shift right into my morning routine with complete joy and excitement.

Wherever you are in your journey, find a bit of time—even if it's just a minute of conscious thought when you are in the shower or driving—to acknowledge all the positivity in your life. Even if you are grappling with what feels like a difficult time of challenges or obstacles, focusing on the things that are working will strengthen their vibration and help you keep moving in your desired direction.

Exercise: Checklist Manifesto

In the early stages of my own transformation journey, I created a spreadsheet entitled "Ways of Being," and I filled it with just that—the ways I was going to live every single day in order to achieve my goals. Not only did this give me a structured way to envision and set my goals, but it also gave me a little dopamine rush every time I checked something off! I did it for 30 days, and at the end I had marks on every single goal, every single day, and I was well on my way to long-lasting transformation. You can get there too!

Try this for yourself. Create a checklist grid and include the ways of being that are in line with your soul map. Here are some suggestions for your list:

- Spend time reading a book instead of watching TV.
- Replace an unhealthy meal with a big salad.
- Drink one to two juices daily. (Focus on the ratio we talked about earlier, leaning more towards veggies to keep your body running optimally.)

- Move your body for at least 20 minutes each day. (This can be anything you enjoy, like chasing your kids around, hiking, yoga—whatever your heart desires.)
- Reconnect with friends you've been neglecting, and rekindle those relationships!
- Make your bed every morning. (You'll be surprised how this sets your day up for success.)
- Compliment someone.
- Begin and end your day by stating in writing or aloud three things you are grateful for.

Chapter 8

BUILD MOMENTUM

At this point I'd say you owe yourself a nice big pat on the back. You've come a long way, through challenging stretches of darkness. Now I want to share with you some additional tools and ways of being that will help you continue building on the incredible investment you have put into yourself through the last several chapters. These techniques will help you build momentum, create your new reality, and ensure that you have so much conviction and faith in this new version of yourself that you'll be able to crush whatever challenges arise for you in the future.

Trusting Your Inner Guide

Remember all that work we did to identify your limitations and to reverse the childhood conditioning that has been keeping your light locked away deep within you? Underneath all that lies your true self and your connection to your knowingness, your intuition. We've all got it—it's an inherent, permanent part of each one of us. Some of us are able to act upon our intuition better than others, however, because we each have different degrees of faith in it. Maybe you grew up in a family where the emphasis was on science, on the analytical powers of the left brain. If this is the case, it's quite possible your education did not encourage your belief in your own intuition. Or maybe you were raised with a heavy dose of religion, where faith and belief were important but entirely dictated to you, and where any questioning was frowned upon. If either of these was your experience, your faith in your intuition is likely to be a little shaky. So how do you put all that away and plug back into the incredible power of your intuition?

Dreamwork

One way to plug into your intuition is to use the power of your dreams. (They don't call me Woo-Woo-Drew for nothing!) Dreams are a very powerful source of information. They draw upon parts of your brain you don't normally have access to when you're awake. Of course, the information is often encoded, but with belief and a bit of organization, you'll be able to figure out the code and tap into this rich resource.

One easy way to begin to connect with your dreams is by recording them in a journal. Keep a notebook by your bedside and when you wake up, write down everything you can remember. Record not only the sights and the sounds but also the feelings involved. Record your waking reactions also. Are you surprised that a certain person or place appeared? Don't worry about coming up with a specific analysis for each dream every day. Over time you will notice patterns and themes. Take these seriously—your intuition is trying to get your attention!

The next step is to begin asking questions of your dreaming self. I do this every night—I call it night school. Just before I drift off to sleep, I direct a question to my subconscious. Not my idea—Thomas Edison said, "Never go to sleep without a request to your subconscious." I'm going to go out on a limb and say it worked pretty well for him! And personally, I couldn't agree more with this manifestation practice. So send those questions in and give your sleeping brain something to mull over. In the morning as you're making an entry in your journal, pay special attention to whether or not you received something useful in response. Don't skip the things that may seem insignificant. In my experience those small signs are often the stepping stones to the big stuff!

Now that you're establishing a link between your waking self and your sleeping self, you can make it even stronger by committing to take a bit of control. As you get more and more in touch with your dreams and your subconscious, you'll get more comfortable with that layer of your consciousness and then you can begin to exercise some willpower. Think of how powerful it would be if you could will yourself to start having dreams that would help you along your transformation journey. I want you to commit to having such dreams, using the tools of intention and clarity of purpose just as you did in vision casting in the last chapter. Dream yourself into that new environment you might be needing, or dream your way past your limitations. In the dream realm, the possibilities are endless. So take advantage of those aspects of yourself that are normally locked away during waking hours to aid you, and add their power to your light.

Body Scan

In the moments just before sleep, you can talk to your body. Every night when I'm lying in bed, I send my awareness down through my body, searching for pain, discomfort, or anything else that needs attention. Let's say I find pain in my knee—I ask it what it needs from me. Oftentimes the pain will lessen just with that act of attention. And if I need to take further steps to heal myself, I know have that awareness.

Meditation

Meditation is a technique that arises in many different cultures and takes on many different forms, but the goal is largely the same—to cut through the static of a racing, doubting mind and get you in touch with the deeper, clearer parts of your being. Some traditions call for long periods of motionless sitting while focusing on a mantra or a specific image. Others look to clear the mind entirely. Still others use movement to keep the mind present and rooted, as with tai chi. Whatever the form, meditation's health benefits are backed by extensive scientific research. The active practice of mindfulness lowers stress levels and blood pressure and speeds up healing. And with those benefits, of course, comes a stronger connection to your authentic self. Do a little reading and experimentation to find a method that works for you, and commit to a regular practice!

How do you know if a particular meditation practice is working? As you develop your new meditation routine, focus on the movement of your mind. See its workings as if they were the surface of the sea. Your busy mind is like the water on a windy day—lots of movement, waves, and foam. Maybe you're replaying events of your day or obsessing over something that happened the day before. Maybe you're worried about something in the future or maybe you just have an annoying jingle from a radio ad looping through your thoughts and adding to the chaos. All this makes it impossible to see what lies beneath the surface. Your deeper thoughts and the larger currents in your life are entirely obscured by all that surface commotion.

The act of meditation will settle that surface, allowing you access to what lies beneath. It works through the very simple process of recognition—you separate your being just enough from your racing thoughts to be able to look at them and notice they are there, and then you let them go. In essence, you create a more stable version of your consciousness that exists separately from all those busy daily thoughts.

If you practice with enough regularity, your whole thought process will begin to change. All the noise and chatter will begin to decrease, leaving you calmer, steadier, more at peace, and more in touch with your intuition. Experiment with a few different methods, and when you find one that resonates with your journey, make it a part of your daily routine.

Something to remember, and something you may not have heard much about, is that meditation does not have to be a quiet-minded experience to be effective. As you are well aware, we live in a loud, go-go-go society. Meditation is less about judging the commotion in your mind than creating the awareness that it exists and allowing yourself permission to release things as they come in while you are working to cultivate more tranquility in your mind space.

You Be You Challenge: The 10-Day Intuition Exercise

We are going to embark on a journey to specifically expand upon and harness the power of your new dreamwork and meditation techniques. I invite you to keep a dream journal for the next 10 days. Every morning when you wake up, take a few minutes to jot down what you remember about your dreams and a few more minutes to reflect upon how they made you feel. Then I want you to really sit with these emotions and think about what your intuition might be telling you. Every night write down requests for your dreaming mind to work on. Perhaps you're looking for answers to particular questions or guidance on a decision. Assign these questions to your sleeping mind, and in the morning notice if any of those requests have been answered.

In addition, commit to a meditation practice for those 10 days. For the first three days, try a few different methods. Perhaps one day you could sit on the floor and focus on a mantra, and another day you could sit in a straight-backed chair with your feet flat on the floor and focus on your breath, and another day you might try a walking meditation, which is a very slow walk with your attention focused completely on the deliberate movements of your body. If the weather and your surroundings invite you, incorporate nature into your practice—perhaps you've got a bench in your garden or a path through some nearby woods. Keep these experiments short—5 or 10 minutes should do it. You need just enough time to gather some data on which one seems most effective at calming your mind. After your three-day experiment, pick the meditation method you like the most and repeat it for the next seven days, striving to be as regular and consistent as you can. Remember, there is no room for judgment in this process. There is no "right" way to do this. The goal is to find what works for you, allowing you to drop into your heart and spirit and practice quieting your mind enough to tune in to Source, your subconscious mind, and your authentic self.

At the end of those 10 days, ask yourself these questions: Do you feel more centered in your mind, body, and soul? Have you discovered hidden desires and new ideas or had epiphanies that had been clouded by your monkey mind? (That's just another way of saying "busy mind.") Do you feel calmer? Do you feel like you have more faith in your intuition? If the answer to all these questions is yes—and I bet it is—then think of how you'll feel after another ten days, and then after another hundred, and then after a thousand. The time investment is minimal for the abundance you will receive in cultivating such a powerful habit each day.

Fail Forward

Okay here's the deal—I am calling this section "Fail Forward" because it's catchy and I think it will help you remember its lessons, but I'm immediately going to backtrack on that, because I don't believe in failure and I want you to get yourself to a place where you don't either. "Failure" only arises if there is an ending to the story, and the story only ends if you give up—and nobody's giving up here, right?

Of course, things are not always going to go as planned. No matter how clear your vision, no matter how strong your intention, there will always be factors beyond your ability to control or predict, including your own very human self. This is especially true as you get farther along in your journey and start developing the confidence to take greater risks—which are a critical part of stretching yourself to get outside your comfort zone and broaden the possibilities for your life.

There will be missteps and dead ends along the course of your journey. But what do you do if you hit a dead end while driving to an important meeting, date, or other event? Do you give up and head back home? I am betting not. You retrace your steps until you're back on course and you start again in a new direction. But guess what? You learned something while on the wrong path. You learned what not to do, where not to go. You might have even discovered something new in a part of town you never intended to visit, and while it isn't your immediate destination, it might be something you'll file away to revisit later. Everything has a purpose—even the "whoops" moments, both big and small.

How does this relate to real life? Let's say you're just emerging from a difficult relationship. People like to talk about relationships "failing," but not you, my friend. You survived, and you lived through a time that held many lessons for you about love, about yourself, and about life in general. Maybe those lessons are hard to see when you're in the midst of the immediate emotional turmoil, but with some time, attention, and self-compassion, you will find a great deal of benefit to carry with you into your next relationship.

Believe me, I know all about this. My own childhood conditioning and my struggles with self-worth have made romantic relationships a little more challenging for me at times and have led me to question and doubt myself even more. But each time I learn more about myself and I'm able to bring a little more understanding and compassion to my journey.

Another example might be a job interview that didn't quite go the way you hoped. Maybe you thought you were fully prepared and had the right experiences and skills. But then you found out in the interview that you were missing something the employer was really looking for. Well, you've learned something valuable, and now you can use that information to decide whether you should seek a different type of employment or get that missing skill or experience so you can come back again better than before. Or let's say you go through a series of interviews and they all go beautifully, but then you find out somebody else got the job. Here too is a valuable lesson—you know that you are absolutely on the right track, and what's more, you've honed your interviewing skills and given your confidence levels a boost. You have no ability to control what kind of competition you're up against, so if that employer found a candidate who seemed to be a better match at the time, what does that have to do with you? Nothing whatsoever! Take that progress you made, convert it to encouragement, use it to propel yourself forward, and consider yourself blessed to have had the opportunity to share positive interactions with new people.

Some missteps are going to hurt more than others, of course. The risks you take will carry different degrees of importance and different degrees of emotion. Some of the dead ends are only going to throw you off a few minutes, but others are going to demand a lot more time and energy and maybe even some creativity before the sting goes away. But the process is the same in each case. So keep your thoughts aligned with your most essential purpose, draw upon your commitment, and keep working to find your way through. And remember, there's always somebody who's been through it before. There is help for whatever stage of the journey you find yourself struggling with. Don't be afraid to ask for it.

Enthusiasm: What Is It?

You know the word *enthusiasm*, of course, but do you know what it *really* means? At its core is the Greek word *theos*, which means "god." From that root we get the Greek word *enthous*, which means "possessed by a god." The word's sacred meaning has been lost over time, but now you can bring it back! The next time you're feeling enthusiasm for something, realize you're in the grip of divine inspiration—and use that realization to make yourself unstoppable!

Become Your Own Biggest Fan

There will be times when you can't find a helping hand, and that will be okay too, if you can remain your own biggest fan. I'd like to share with you a visualization exercise that helps me stay positive when I've got to rely on myself for a boost. It comes from the book *The Trophy Effect* by Michael Nitti, a good friend and mentor of mine. The trophy effect is a subconscious bias that leads us to focus on our shortcomings rather than our accomplishments. Counteracting this effect requires conscious effort, like the following visualization.

Here's how it works: First, imagine a trophy room, like something from high school. You know the type—a great big wood-paneled room full of steel racks holding trophies of every size and shape. If you went to a high school like mine, there were a bunch of small trophies for the swim club, medium-sized ones for the cross-country team, and an *enormous* one the football team won at the state championship.

Got that image in your mind? Good! Now on every trophy imagine something *you've done yourself* etched into that shiny brass finish. Assign small accomplishments to the small trophies, like, *I didn't yell at that guy who cut me off in traffic.* Assign more and more significant accomplishments to the bigger trophies, giving yourself credit for things like . . .

- Calling your parents
- Maintaining your finances
- Picking your kids up from school on time
- Being consistent in doing your housework
- Getting a promotion at work
- Trying something new
- Getting your roof fixed
- Doing something on your bucket list

These are all important and all worthy of celebration. Imagine all the achievements you can think of etched onto those trophies. Now, in your imagination, stand up and look around your trophy room. That trophy room is yours alone, and you deserve to take joy in it. You know why? Because all those things are true!

Finally, consider the one common denominator to all these accomplishments: *you.* You picked yourself up and did all those things. Sure, you had some help and encouragement along the way, but *your* decisions, *your* efforts, and *your* persistence created all those achievements.

That's your past—now let's look to your future to make sure the trophy room keeps expanding. Pick three things that you've been putting off or struggling to find the motivation to complete. Imagine an empty shelf in the trophy room, just big enough for three trophies, of whatever size they need to be. Now, for each one, make the following declaration:

I commit to _____ *, and when I accomplish this, I will celebrate by* _____ .

Choose a celebration that matches the accomplishment. And don't forget to add that trophy to your case when you're finished.

Whenever you need to lift yourself up, return to this visualization and review all those trophy labels. That's *you*, and it demonstrates all you're capable of. Use that thought to keep your momentum through whatever life decides to throw at you next.

Intuitive Eating

With all this great work you're doing to level up your mind and soul, don't forget to remain consciously aware of making healthy food choices to fuel your body too! The next time you're looking at a menu, think about how you've wired your brain for making decisions. Instead of choosing food for the way it will taste in the moment, tune in to your body's deeper systems and ask, *Body, what do you need from me now?* Be present for the response, and then ask yourself, *How is this meal going to make me feel three hours from now?* So often we make choices on autopilot, but with this bit of mindfulness, I'll bet that menu suddenly looks different! And yes, food should still taste good. You can have both—it may just take a little trial and error to find what works best for your personal goals.

You Be You Challenge: Recommit to the Ride

For this challenge pick something from your past that you gave up on because it didn't go quite how you hoped it would or because it took more effort than you were willing to make at the time. This might have been a relationship, a weight-loss goal, or a career plan—for instance, maybe you set aside a career to have a family or took some sort of exam that produced discouraging results.

This challenge is simple—go try again! And don't just think about it either. Writing things down is a powerful tool to keep the momentum of your dreams and goals in the forefront, so declare what it is you want to recommit to and then decide on the steps you are going to take within X number of days. Remember that there are plenty of people in your circle who want to see you crush your limitations, so this is a great time to lean on them and ask for what you need to succeed. Keep building upon your action steps until you see your commitment realized. And don't forget to celebrate!

Through this book you've learned new ways of being and discovered some of the blind spots that kept you from succeeding in the past, so you'll be able to approach the endeavor with a new perspective. I'd wish you luck—but with your commitment and new skills, you won't need it!

Chapter 9

TAP INTO SOURCE

Here we are at the final step of the *You Be You* transformation journey! You've come a tremendous distance, and if you've followed the guidance of this program, you know with certainty that things will never again be as they were before you started. You've seen at least glimpses of your brilliant light, and you've had a taste of what you get to do to make sure it shines brightly for all your remaining days on this earth, and well beyond. While much of the work you've done has been task-oriented—the body cleanse, journaling, experiments in meditation, and so on—this final step is of a more spiritual nature. Before we part ways, I want to make sure there's absolutely no question that your transformation is *not* just about you getting what you want or being who you want. I believe with all my being that instead this is a sacred journey, the creation of a foundation you can use to lift up your family, your friends, and your whole community, with the effects rippling out to all humanity. And when you create the best possible existence for yourself, you do the same for those around you, and this, to me, is what plugging into Source, honoring God, is all about. This chapter will focus on this connection and strive to cement this mind-set within you, so that as you move forward, you'll carry this sense with you.

My Definition of *Source*

Source, or the light, is that which we all share, the oneness that exists beyond our human form, beyond the 3-D bodies we've been given to inhabit in this lifetime. It is the single unified light that shines into, through, and out from each one of us. Some people call it God; other people have different names for it. Whatever the label, it is the pure love and unity all living things share. And you are very much a part of that equation.

Throughout your journey nothing will help you more—help you stay committed, help you be compassionate to yourself, help you stay in alignment with your deepest purpose—than remembering to maintain your connection to Source. In religious traditions this is called praying, and it's direct communication with God. In other traditions it takes many forms. It could be meditation or other practices that help you stay grounded and rooted to your body, to the earth, to those around you, and to the greater good.

That connection with the divine is 100 percent real, and it is absolutely yours to claim. All you have to do is believe you are worthy—and you are! Your self-compassion and self-acceptance bring you right into that light, infusing every part of you, even (especially!) those parts of you you're working to transform.

This means loving yourself, top to bottom. It means accepting that you're human, and that it's okay to mess up, for things not to go your way, to be messy. It means giving yourself permission to release your baggage, whether physical weight or financial issues or relationship struggles. It means letting go of any last pieces of shame or guilt. It means knowing you are perfectly imperfect, completely unique yet part of that greater oneness. It means knowing that you are loved and accepted exactly as you are, because you were created with purpose, and that you're on the path that will take you to all the places you want to go. Your desires are not without a deeper meaning, so choose to trust. And know that the path may not look the way you imagined, but ultimately the Universe is continuously conspiring in your favor—even in the dark moments that feel a little scary, and maybe even unmanageable or impossible to overcome.

You Are the One

How much responsibility are you taking for the life you are living right now? I am not asking this with judgment—rather, it's a question I encourage you to get brutally honest about. The life you are living is yours, and the cold, hard truth is that it's up to you to create that which you desire. Each day you have a choice as to how you will show up. Each moment is a new opportunity to step into alignment with who you are now and who you are working to become. With that, I will ask you again . . . how much responsibility are you taking for the life you are living right now?

This is your chance to choose differently—better, maybe. If the life you are living isn't all you want it to be, it's time to tap into Source, the place inside you where your truth resides, and embrace it fully. There is no better time than now to own your light and celebrate all the potential still untapped, begging for you to share. You, my friend, are the One.

Now, before you assume I have gone absolutely crazy, listen up! You know by now that we are all connected, right? You, me, the Universe, all of it. And you also know by now, especially after reading this book, that there is a ton of room for expansion and growth and evolution, both individually and collectively, yes? Do you also understand the power you have to create meaningful and fulfilling change in your own environment as well as the environment around you? It's massive! Simply put . . .

You are the One.

And that said, you are the only thing standing in the way between where you are now and where you want to go. Maybe that feels like a foreign concept, although hopefully by this point, it's beginning to resonate a little deeper with you. My hope is that through this journey you have also been practicing flipping the script on your limiting beliefs and you're able to take that initial thought and transform it into something that feels powerful and exciting! Because guess what? You've totally got this!

Now is the time to own the power you have in your experience and give yourself a big pat on the back for the life you are surely rocking in this moment. It's also the perfect time to welcome new opportunities, because I can promise you they will come. In fact, they have probably already begun to roll in. You have the power, my friend. You get to create anything you want in this lifetime. I will say it again . . . *you* are the *One.*

Reconnecting to Source

When I think of Source—God, our light, that over-arching oneness that holds us all together—I often think of the story of Jackie. Jackie came to me "broken" (as she referred to herself). She'd recently lost her husband, Gordon, to cancer, after 20 years together. The last few months of his life were heartbreaking. She expressed her heartache about watching a once strong, indepen-dent, and active man become unable to do anything for himself—even things we take for granted like using the bathroom or picking up a fork to eat. She'd lie next to him at night, wide awake, wondering if this would be the night he'd take his last breath. She wanted to savor every moment she had left, even the dark moments, which proved to be harder than she could ever have imagined.

Jackie had always believed in something bigger than herself, but she was far from religious. And despite the hardship of her husband's passing, she was surrounded by love. Her daughter, Olivia, was a constant support, reminding her that she didn't have to go through this alone, reminding her that the Universe was holding its arms open wide to receive Gordon, as well as to hold Jackie as she continued to wake up every day and choose to live. It was up to Jackie whether or not she would accept this love and support, and ultimately, she did.

I met Jackie by chance, if you can really call it that. It was divine timing, that's for sure. She wasn't a client, but she was definitely a soul I was meant to meet when I did. The Universe is funny like that. Jackie taught me a thing or two about what it really means to live. And in our conversations, through tears and even with some anger toward her situation, she continued to rise. While I was trying to console her, she was the one reminding me what a gift it was to be alive. I admired her strength and perseverance. I was drawn to her vulnerable heart and her drive to move through her pain.

It was during this time that Jackie "invited in" Source (again, her words). She made the choice to trust that everything in her path had meaning in life and in death. We discussed Gordon and laughed about some of his funny habits and the things that once drove her crazy that she now missed, like the way he had talked to himself as he cooked and the way he interrupted her when he felt really passionate about something. But mostly she missed his rough hands and warm heart, his companionship, more than anything and was still trying to wrap her mind around the fact that the life they had planned together would no longer be possible. I asked her where her drive to keep going in such a beautiful and positive way came from, and she said something so simple yet so profound: "It's a choice."

How many times have you faced a difficult situation and found yourself in so much pain, sadness, or any other emotion that didn't feel good, that you could just not fathom how on earth you could possibly keep going? I know I've been there. And in the end how'd you get out of it? Choice, right? You chose to do something about it, whether it was to seek professional help or something else entirely. My point is, you didn't have to go through it on your own. And even in moments when you might have felt isolated and that nobody understood you, Source, the Universe, God, whomever or whatever you resonate with, had your back.

Believing this as truth is your call, of course. But I will say that in my experience and in the experience of others I have met and worked with, this rings true. When you decide to give up the false idea that you have to do everything all alone or that you are hopelessly destined to a certain life or body or job forever, a light comes on. *Your* light. Because in that moment, whether consciously or not, you are communicating with Source and saying, "I'm ready to rise!" And that is always rewarded in one way or another.

Maybe you can relate to Jackie's story. Maybe you have lost someone or something that mattered to you deeply. My heart goes out to you. And at the same time, I also know you will come out on the other side and your light will shine again, my friend. You are here now, and that means you have fought to be here somehow. Maybe you are still fighting. And that's inspiring.

Trust the Process

Trust the process, including the timing of it all. Easier said than done sometimes, isn't it? Consider this, though: how much energy do you expend trying to control everything that happens in your life? It can get exhausting! I'll admit, releasing control used to be a big challenge for me. Sometimes it still comes up, but my awareness around it has allowed me to notice when it's an issue and choose better. Have you ever found yourself trying to control a situation you knew you could not possibly change, but what the heck, you were up for the challenge anyway? I know you have; you're human! Me too. Talk about a waste of energy!

Surrendering and trusting that all will unfold perfectly is such a powerful practice for so many reasons. First off, there are so many things to accomplish! We can't possibly believe that we can do all of it on our own, in our own timing, and get the results we truly want. When we surrender to the process, we are telling the Universe that we are willing to trust the plan that has been laid out. This doesn't mean we are going to sit back and eat bonbons as we wait for everything to fall into our laps. What it does mean, though, is that we are tuning in to the Universe's signals and consciously making decisions based on the things that feel most congruent with our commitment to ourselves.

Secondly, trusting the process allows space for more good to unfold. It creates more quiet moments to be with ourselves and those around us. It provides a calmness to know (to trust) that we really are supported. And that feels amazing!

If you've been betrayed and trust feels uncomfortable or scary or brings up emotions that leave you anxious, acknowledge them. These moments can be great practice in gratitude. Send out a big fat *thank you* to the Universe, because these are the moments when Source is showing you where your growth opportunities still lie and what places still need to heal.

Trust is just another muscle to practice daily. So with each new experience, consider asking yourself how you can let go a little more to create more space for more good to show up. Where are you holding on so tightly that thinking about it creates a deep-rooted sensation in your body? This is your starting point. This is where you get to practice the art of release—and where you get to feel the freedom that follows.

Exercise: Forgive Yourself . . . for Everything

There is enough pain, suffering, and sadness in the world. Instead of adding to all that by focusing on your past, I am inviting you to be part of the solution. I am inviting you to work with me to inspire hope in others, because you are now proof of all that's possible.

Thinking about forgiving yourself can feel a little uncomfortable, especially if the wounds are fresh. That's okay. Acknowledge the emotions. Honor them. And then, you guessed it . . . *let them go*. Forgiveness is not about saying what happened was right or wrong; it's about freeing yourself from the prison of shame, guilt, anger, anxiety—all the emotions that do not serve your highest self. You can think of forgiveness as a rite of passage, in a way, because I promise you there are whole worlds on the other side if you can bring yourself to feel and say, "This happened, but I am stronger and better for it." (Whatever "this" may be!)

I want you to grab a piece of paper. Light some candles and sit in silence with yourself and all your thoughts. Let them come in and out of your mind space fluidly, just like a rolling river. Allow your heart to expand as each memory flows in, even the ones that don't feel particularly good. Remember, the "bad" moments are just as valuable and necessary to your path as the ones you deem "good." With each thought that doesn't serve you, say aloud, "Thank you for your role in my experience. I release you. I am free." Do this over and over until all you feel is love. It may happen quickly or it may take some time. There's no right way, no wrong way. Simply be as you are, judgment-free and present.

If it feels right for you, write down each memory that gets stuck on repeat in the vortex of your mind. Sometimes the act of writing things down can have more power to break the tie we have to them. Write them out with the same surrender statement, but also say it aloud: "Thank you for your role in my experience. I release you. I am free." Do this as many times as you need to until you feel the euphoria of having a clean slate to create new experiences and call in new opportunities and people.

Now take a deep breath, smile, and know you are free, my friend. Free to be *you*, just as you are.

CONCLUSION

We're in This Together

You made it! You are doing the work, and because of that there's no doubt in my mind that your life will shift in a way that feels better and more aligned with your authentic self. Maybe it has shifted already! But this is only the beginning. The real work is in how you choose to show up each day—that is, your thoughts and actions. Every day is a new opportunity to say yes to yourself in a way that brings you closer to the you that has been silenced for far too long.

Every time you choose yourself, you are giving others permission to do the same. As we all do more of this, we begin to shift the consciousness of humanity, and I believe that by using the universal language of love, we can absolutely shift the world. It may not happen overnight, but anything worth having takes time, right? The important thing is that there's hope, and by showing up and sharing the gifts that have been bestowed upon you, you are contributing in a positive way to a better world, a more meaningful existence for future generations. And if enough of us create a lifelong commitment to this goal, together we can lift each other up and create the power to transform the world for the better.

Seems easy enough in principle, doesn't it? So why, then, do we experience so much separateness in our everyday lives? Why do so many of us struggle to come together? Why do we create so many ways—from national borders and religious affiliations all the way down to sports team loyalties—to divide one group from one another? Why do we fight? Why do we experience envy?

I believe there are a few causes for this. The first is obvious—we each inhabit a separate body. Our most immediate perception of the world is through our own eyes and ears and fingertips, and it becomes clear to us as small children that the world I am seeing at any one time is different than the world you are perceiving at that time, because we both cannot be in the exact same physical space at once.

We also have leftover instincts from ancient human history at work here, when resources were scarce and tribalism helped us survive. If my hunting grounds were just enough to sustain me and my tribe, then any other hunters in that area were a direct threat to my life and my family's lives. So it was necessary to focus on differences, and part of that was the need to dehumanize others. If I thought too long and hard about how that other hunter was just trying to feed his own family, I'd reach a level of empathy that would actually hurt my chances of getting myself and my family through the winter.

The world has obviously changed tremendously since those days, but that sort of tribalism is still rampant. Nearly all the conflict in the world is conducted between those who label themselves one way and those who label themselves in a different way. We see this across religions, ethnicities, political belief systems, and so on. And what makes this even worse is the fact that our leaders exploit this aspect of our collective psychology to control us. If we can be made to fear other people, then we will follow—and vote for—those who claim to be able to protect us. If we can be made to live in fear, we will expend all our energy fighting the other guy, and we will have no energy left to see through all the lies and misinformation.

But what would happen if enough people could see all those differences, all that fear for the manipulative lies they are, and begin to make decisions from a place of love and unity? We'd put the politicians out of business. We'd end so many of the debates that exhaust our time and energy, because we would know the way we take care of ourselves is by taking care of other people, and any ideologies to the contrary would be exposed for the fear and the selfishness they are based on.

How do we get there? It starts with us—you and me. It starts with the realization that on a soul level, we are connected, that every "thing" and every "being" on the planet is here in this moment and all moments, together, sharing energetic space and creating the world we are each experiencing. It starts with accepting nothing less than the best versions of ourselves as we walk into the world each day. It starts with taking radical action and committing to our own personal work and sharing what we've learned. In this way we can create a revolution of love and togetherness, a mass of light that will beat back the shadows that not only have been lurking inside us but that have fallen across the world.

My hope is that this book has inspired you to think bigger, do better, and believe that it's all possible. Because it absolutely is.

And with that, I've just got one final thing to say to you—it's something I've said before, but after the journey we've been through in these pages, I think you'll understand completely when I say it: *We are*—now and forever, through all times and all dimensions, for the betterment of this shared life—*in this together.*

That's enough out of me! This journey isn't about me, after all—it's about *you.* So I want to wrap up with a few ways for you to check back in with yourself and to keep the momentum going once you turn the final page of this book.

Exercise: Awesomeness Audit, Part Two

Remember that awesomeness audit you took at the beginning of this book? I want you to take it again so you can show yourself how far you've come. Don't look at your earlier answers quite yet—instead, run through the items and score them a second time. Remember, you're scoring your satisfaction levels, using a 1 to 5 scale (1 = not satisfied, 5 = extremely satisfied). Again, be completely honest, and do this with love and self-acceptance, with no judgment of your own journey—if you haven't experienced a shift in some area, we'll address that in a moment! Here are the areas again:

- Friends
- Romantic partnership/relationship
- Career
- Finances
- Health/body
- Home/family life
- Spiritual path

Now pull out the answers from your first time through the exercise and compare your new answers to them. I'm willing to bet you're rocking a big smile right about now, looking at that evidence of your transformation already taking shape. Keep it going!

But what if you don't see a lot of change? That's absolutely okay. This stuff isn't easy, and everybody has their own journey. First, stay in that place of love and acceptance for yourself and your process. Run through the experiments and exercises again, taking it slow and being patient. You'll get there, I promise!

Exercise: Commit to Yourself . . . Again

Let's also go back to that commitment you made to your transformation in Chapter 1. Now that you've come as far as you have, let's do it again—with one small modification. In the last stages of this journey, we've been discussing how a commitment to yourself is a commitment to other people too, so let's update that official statement to your membership in our growing revolution of love!

I, _____ [your name here], commit to _____ [three to five ways of being] because I love myself so much that I want _____ [desire] for myself and I believe it's possible because I said so. I recognize that this commitment will not only bring me to my highest self but will also lift up all those around me, inspiring them to attain their highest selves. In this way we will _____ [goal for the planet] together.

Signature _____

Date _____

Finally . . .

One last exercise, and then it's your turn to head out and be a role model for personal transformation! Remember that photo you took of yourself at the beginning of the journey? Get it out and sit with it. Bring up all the self-compassion and self-love you've been working on and direct it at that version of yourself. Thank yourself for arriving at the beginning of this process. Take another photograph of yourself now and take a look at them side by side. Note any differences you feel between your current self and that earlier version. Simply acknowledge them and let that inform your feelings about your journey. Finally, put both photos away, take a deep breath, stand up, and go out there and *shine*!

ACKNOWLEDGMENTS

I want to acknowledge my dear friend, Sheree Trask, for brainstorming with me on the message within and contributing to this book. To Jason Buchholz, for helping *You Be You* come to life. And to my Organifi family for their continuous love and support in this human experience. I love you all.

ABOUT THE AUTHOR

Drew Canole is a rock star in the world of fitness, nutrition, and mind-set, with a huge heart for others and doing his part to transform the world, one person at a time. As the founder of Fitlife.tv, he is committed to sharing educational, inspirational, and entertaining videos and articles about health, fitness, healing, and longevity. Drew believes that people are at their best when challenged. He pushes others to bust through personal barriers and reach new heights in physical, mental, and spiritual well-being.

Websites: fitlife.tv, organifi.com

We hope you enjoyed this Hay House book. If you'd like to receive our online catalog featuring additional information on Hay House books and products, or if you'd like to find out more about the Hay Foundation, please contact:

Hay House, Inc., P.O. Box 5100, Carlsbad, CA 92018-5100
(760) 431-7695 or (800) 654-5126
(760) 431-6948 (fax) or (800) 650-5115 (fax)
www.hayhouse.com® • www.hayfoundation.org

———

Published in Australia by: Hay House Australia Pty. Ltd.,
18/36 Ralph St., Alexandria NSW 2015
Phone: 612-9669-4299 • *Fax:* 612-9669-4144
www.hayhouse.com.au

Published in the United Kingdom by: Hay House UK, Ltd.,
The Sixth Floor, Watson House, 54 Baker Street, London W1U 7BU
Phone: +44 (0)20 3927 7290 • *Fax:* +44 (0)20 3927 7291
www.hayhouse.co.uk

Published in India by: Hay House Publishers India,
Muskaan Complex, Plot No. 3, B-2, Vasant Kunj, New Delhi 110 070
Phone: 91-11-4176-1620 • *Fax:* 91-11-4176-1630
www.hayhouse.co.in

———

Access New Knowledge.
Anytime. Anywhere.

Learn and evolve at your own pace
with the world's leading experts.

www.hayhouseU.com

Listen. Learn. Transform.

Listen to the audio version of this book for FREE!

Today, life is more hectic than ever—so you deserve on-demand and on-the-go solutions that inspire growth, center your mind, and support your well-being.

Introducing the *Hay House Unlimited Audio* mobile app. Now you can listen to this book (and countless others)—without having to restructure your day.

With your membership, you can:

- Enjoy over 30,000 hours of audio from your favorite authors.

- Explore audiobooks, meditations, Hay House Radio episodes, podcasts, and more.

- Listen anytime and anywhere with offline listening.

- Access exclusive audios you won't find anywhere else.

Try FREE for 7 days!

Visit hayhouse.com/unlimited to start your free trial and get one step closer to living your best life.